Developing the

Survival Attitude

By
Phil L. Duran

LOOSELEAF LAW PUBLICATIONS, INC.
41-23 150th Street
Flushing, NY 11355

(ISBN 1-889031-14-3)

This book is dedicated to every person
joining the ranks of law enforcement
who is determined to survive
through skill and attitude.

Acknowledgments

I would like to thank my wife, Gay,
for all her support and encouragement.

About the Author

Phil Duran has been a law enforcement officer since 1988. He is certified by the state of New Mexico as an Officer Survival instructor. He has received training in Officer Survival from the Bernalillo County Sheriff's Department, the New Mexico Law Enforcement Academy, and the Federal Bureau of Investigation. He holds an instructor certificate in Officer Survival from the Metropolitan Police Institute in Miami, Florida. He has been published in Law and Order magazine on the subject of Officer Survival. Phil Duran is also certified by the state of New Mexico as an instructor in general police subjects, bombs and explosives, and booby trap devices. His experience includes patrol, court services, and academy assignments. He knows first hand what it means to be involved in a critical incident, and what it takes to survive, including the importance of the proper attitude and how it relates to survival.

Table of Contents

ii

"He may be a very nice man. But I haven't got the time to figure that out. All I know is, he's got a uniform and a gun and I have to relate to him that way. That's the only way to relate to him because one of us may have to die."

James Baldwin (1924-87), U.S. author

Introduction

If you are interested in joining the ranks of law enforcement, or have already done so, this book is for you. It is my hope that this book will provide you with the basics that you need to develop the proper attitude necessary for survival on patrol, or in any other law enforcement assignment. It makes no difference whatsoever, if you are joining as a volunteer member of a reserve organization, or as a full-time, salaried peace officer. Anyone who is involved in law enforcement faces the same dangers. When someone decides to launch an attack against you, that person neither knows, nor cares, if you are on the payroll or not. You will be seen only as an officer of the law, and no different from any other. So you must be prepared.

The same is true of the agency that you decide to join. You may be considering a career with any agency ranging from your local home town police or sheriff's department to a branch of the federal government, such as the Drug Enforcement Administration or the Federal Bureau of Investigation. In any case, you will be carrying a badge and a gun, and you will be charged with the responsibility of enforcing the law. Therefore, you will be facing some level of danger, in one form or another, which makes the survival attitude very important to your well-being, regardless of jurisdiction or assignment.

With this in mind, I have provided you with the basics of the survival attitude. These basics can be applied to your particular situation, whatever that may be. Remember that these are only the basics and that this is just the beginning of your education in survival. I could not possibly provide you with everything there is to know about the survival attitude. New ideas are being presented all the time, and that is exactly the way it should be. If we sit back and relax, confident that we know everything that is needed for survival, we will most certainly fail. We must be open minded and eager to accept new ideas and concepts. For this reason, it is just as important for me to continue my education in officer survival as it is for you.

This book is not about tactics or procedures. There are a number of excellent texts available that go into great detail on the subject of tactics. They cover everything from traffic stops to domestic disputes, up to and including tactics to use when involved in a gunfight. Instead, this book is all about the other side of officer survival; the mental aspects, and how they relate to tactics of survival. It is about preparing yourself mentally for the dangers of law enforcement. It is about developing a survival attitude. You cannot depend on good tactics alone to get you through your career. You must have the ability to think tactically, and to prepare yourself mentally for tactical situations.

Please take the concepts in this book, and all training that you receive in your career, very seriously. Law enforcement is a dangerous profession. The National Law Enforcement Officers Memorial in Washington D.C. is a sad testimonial to that fact. The Memorial includes a wall which is inscribed with the names of every law enforcement officer killed in the line of duty in the history of the United States. As sobering a sight as that is, there is something else on the wall that is even more chilling. Large portions of the wall were intentionally left bare when the memorial was dedicated in 1991, to be sure that there is adequate room for the names of all the peace officers that are expected to be killed in the line of duty in the years to come. Thousands and thousands of names will fit in the bare spaces on the wall. It is up to you, and you alone, to ensure that your name is not among them.

"We do not live to think, but, on the contrary,
we think in order that we may succeed in surviving."
José Ortega y Gasset (1883-1955),
Spanish essayist, philosopher

1

The Art of Tactical Thinking

What is tactical thinking? Tactics can be defined as maneuvers, or goal oriented actions. The goal in police work is the safe and successful completion of a specific task, such as a building search, or an arrest. To be tactical can be thought of as the ability to use tactics skillfully even when under pressure. Tactical thinking is the art of understanding every aspect of the use of tactics; from the mental attitude necessary for survival, to the evaluation and assessment of your own tactics.

How then, do you gain this understanding? In order to accomplish this, if you wish to become involved in law enforcement, you must first understand the dangers inherent in police work. It would be very unrealistic to expect someone who does not fully understand the possibility of being killed in the line of duty to be sufficiently concerned about it. Even so, it should not be necessary to use statistics, or case studies, of law enforcement officers killed in the line of duty to convince you that the possibility of death is a grim reality. The fact that law enforcement officers are killed at all, regardless of the numbers, should be sufficient cause for concern for anyone involved in, or interested in, law enforcement. If it isn't, it may be wise to consider a career in some other field.

And law enforcement officers *do* die in the line of duty. In 1992 the Federal Bureau of Investigation released a publication entitled *Killed in the Line of Duty*, in which statistics related to the line of duty deaths of law enforcement officers from 1981 through 1990 were compiled. 762 peace officers were feloniously killed during this ten-year period. Also included are more in-depth studies of selected line of duty deaths that occurred during the same time period. The incidents were studied from a variety of standpoints including profiles of both the offenders and the victim officers, the circumstances surrounding the incidents, the type of weapon used, time of day, and so on.

The FBI also releases a similar publication on a yearly basis called *Law Enforcement Officers Killed and Assaulted*. This yearly publication contains similar studies of all law enforcement officers killed and assaulted during the year previous to publication. Both of these publications contain a wealth of information invaluable to anyone wishing to learn more about the way that officers are killed in the hopes of learning how to prevent line of duty deaths in the future.

The next step is to acquire tactical training from qualified instructors. This is normally done during basic training at a law enforcement training academy, in a controlled environment, and can be supplemented by any of a number of excellent texts available on the subject of tactics and officer survival. In addition, there are numerous magazines geared toward law enforcement, focusing on topics ranging from tactics and training, to administrative issues. While these texts and magazines can be valuable aids in learning the basics of officer survival, they are no substitute for actual instruction by qualified officer survival instructors, and should be used only to supplement such training.

Finally, it is imperative to build on this knowledge base. Law enforcement is a field that provides new and exciting challenges on a daily basis, making it impossible to provide a recruit with a tactic for every possible variation of every possible situation that may be encountered. Once you understand this, you can make the commitment never to stop learning. You should seek out additional training continuously during the course of your career. Officer survival related literature should be studied at every opportunity. Of course, in officer survival training, as in anything else, there is good instruction, and there is bad. Therefore, it is imperative that you have the ability to think for yourself, while never losing sight of the main objective - survival.

A major component of tactical thinking is the ability to take a given tactic, evaluate it, and determine for yourself if the tactic is sound. This requires a bit of experience in addition to basic training. After a relatively short time on the street it will become apparent which tactics make you comfortable or uncomfortable. By understanding which tactics are most favorable, you will begin to develop your own tactical style, which leads to the ability to develop tactics independently. A tactical thinker understands that while some situations require specific tactics and leave little or no room for deviation, many situations call for the ability to adapt quickly to conditions in the real world, which can be quite different from those encountered in a training environment. New tactics are then created. Some are created as a temporary solution to a situation where a more standard tactic was not desirable for some valid reason, and some as a whole new tactic, to be shared with, and possibly adopted by, others in law enforcement circles.

Obviously, there's a lot to think about when striving to become a tactical thinker, especially when you consider the fact that even a momentary lapse in tactical thinking can have devastating consequences. If you are distracted, even for an instant, you can leave yourself open to a violent assault. This is how many law enforcement officers get themselves into trouble. Others have a more than temporary lapse in tactical thinking and leave themselves vulnerable on a regular basis. This is nothing more than complacency. They do the job day after day without ever having to face their own mortality, and they forget that the job is dangerous at all. Their attitude seems to be, "I've been doing this job for years, and I haven't been shot yet." The flaw in this line of thinking is obvious. You can be violently attacked, in one way or another, at any point during your career, from the first day to the last. Naturally, this necessitates the need for you to be on your toes at all times. Remember that police work has often been described as hours of boredom, interrupted by moments of sheer terror.

While it remains true that some peace officers may never be forced to fire their weapons at anything other than stationary targets during their careers, it is also true that every year law enforcement officers are killed in the line of duty. Furthermore, they are violently assaulted every day (*Law Enforcement Officers Killed and Assaulted*). It is upon these facts that you must base your belief system, if you plan to survive a career of twenty years or more. You must plan and prepare for the day *when*, not if, you become involved in a life threatening encounter. This is the only way to be truly prepared for involvement in a critical incident. You must believe that it *will* happen during your career. If you truly believe this, the question in your mind will be, "*When* is it going to happen to me?" rather than "*Will* it happen to me?" or "*What if* it happens to me?" The first question carries the advantage of reinforcing in your mind the fact that at any time you may be faced with a life and death situation. By being continually aware of this, you will be more alert, knowing that each call for service could mean the ultimate test of your training and experience.

An officer who asks, "What if it happens to me?" has not fully accepted the fact that it can happen to him. The only officer less prepared is the one who does not even ask this question, but states confidently, "It won't happen to me." An officer who believes that a critical incident always happens to someone else will never be fully prepared for the day that it happens to him. This is the officer who never takes training seriously. He can usually be found in the back of the room during training sessions, making jokes or doodling on his note pad (if he bothered to bring a pen), or otherwise making his boredom known, regardless of the topic being discussed. He shoots his weapon at the range only when required to do so, and does not feel the need to practice.

His attitude toward training is carried over into his use of tactics and is easily observed by anyone with even minimal training in survival skills. He parks directly in front of the complainant's house when responding to a call, regardless of whether he is there to take a report or investigate a disturbance. He can be seen leaning into the driver's window of a vehicle that he has stopped, as if the driver is someone he has known all his life. He scoffs at those who use good tactics, believing that they are over zealous, and that there is no reason to be the least bit cautious. He never wears body armor because it's too hot, or too uncomfortable, believing that he will die when it's his "time" regardless of how careful he is. It makes me wonder that if he truly believes that he will die when his number is up, and there is nothing he can do to stop it, why then, does he bother to carry a gun?

In spite of all this, he may actually survive a full career of twenty years or more, provided he is never put to the test. If he does survive, it will be due to pure luck rather than skill and attitude, which are the two key components that survival should depend on.

A survival minded officer, on the other hand, understands the importance of training and always takes it seriously. This is the officer that seeks out additional training, and practices his survival skills at every opportunity. He always wears his body armor, regardless of how hot or uncomfortable it can be. He considers a little discomfort to be inconsequential compared to the possibility of a gunshot wound, or wounds. He wears it whether he is assigned to patrol, investigations, or any other assignment, because he knows that as long as he is carrying a badge and a gun, anything can happen. He understands that involvement in life and death encounters is not limited to patrol. Law enforcement officers become involved in critical incidents during a wide variety of assignments, as well as during off-duty hours (*Killed in the Line of Duty*). He wears his body armor not only for himself, but for his family, and for his coworkers. He doesn't want his family and friends to be faced with the loss of a loved one, when the simple act of donning a vest could have spared them the whole ordeal. He also knows that if he fails to wear body armor, and is shot, he may not be able to provide effective backup for his fellow officers. As a tactical thinker he wants to do everything possible to be the best backup he can be.

He never thinks of a burglar alarm call as a "nuisance alarm", regardless of the number of times he has responded to the same address in the past and found it to be false. Instead, he thinks of every alarm as a "good alarm", realizing that the fact that it has been false in the past does not necessarily mean that it will always be a false alarm. He also knows that even if it does turn out to be a false alarm, by treating it as a good alarm and using proper tactics, he has not wasted an opportunity to practice his survival skills. He never makes assumptions about any call. He knows that things are not always as they appear and to make assumptions can be dangerous.

He is able to sense and anticipate danger, and has a planned response ready to put into action if necessary. He continually reassesses his situation and is able to change his plan as the situation dictates. He is aware of everything happening around him, even if it doesn't seem relevant to the situation at hand. He is aware of environmental conditions that affect the existing level of danger, such as traffic hazards. He is aware of his strengths in a given situation and continually weighs them in his assessment of the level of risk involved. He is aware of, and understands, how each of these factors can work for, or against him.

Again, there's a lot to consider. So how does a civilian with limited knowledge of law enforcement become tactically minded? Some may not. At least not to the extent that others will. It is important to understand that tactical thinking appears to be like any other skill, in that it seems to come more naturally to some. No one, however, is born tactically minded. Even the most survival oriented officers had to be taught to think tactically, and must work to maintain a survival attitude.

Your goal, of course, should be to develop a survival attitude that can be maintained throughout an entire career. It's not easy, and it requires a major commitment on your part. Once mastered, however, tactical thinking will become something that you do automatically. Tactical thinkers have a hard time *not* thinking tactically, whether on duty or off. Spouses of law enforcement officers can attest to this, as they witness it on a daily basis. They have learned that they will never again see a movie from any part of the theater other than the back row. They know that if they want to hold hands while strolling down the street they must not hold their spouse's gun-hand. This hand must be kept free in case it's needed. They know that when in a restaurant, an officer will always select the seat that offers the best tactical position, allowing the best view of everything happening in the restaurant, and everyone coming and going, so it's best to let him or her sit first. Perhaps the most annoying survival habit that tactical thinkers possess is the constant observation of everything happening around them. To spouses, this often appears as nothing more than inattention. Of course, all of this constant observation and awareness must be tempered carefully so that it remains in check. Otherwise, simple awareness could deteriorate into paranoia.

With so much to think about it may seem that becoming a tactical thinker is an unattainable goal. Actually, quite the opposite is true. It takes time, dedication, and commitment, but the end result - survival - is well worth the investment.

It is an equal failing to trust everybody,
and to trust nobody.

English Proverb (18th century)

2

Awareness

What type of awareness is necessary for you to become a tactical thinker? Is it self-awareness? Or is it the awareness of your surroundings and all that is taking place? It's both, actually. To be a good tactical thinker, you need to be very aware of how everything that you say and do can affect the situation at hand. Additionally, you must be aware of your surroundings and all the potential dangers that are lurking within.

The first thing that you must become aware of, when venturing into the vast realm of police work, is yourself. It's the little things that can add to, or subtract from, your overall tactical bearing. Starting with the basics, to become a tactically minded officer you must become aware of the noise that you make when you walk, move, or breathe. Being aware of, and controlling the amount of noise that you make is generally referred to as "noise discipline." This may seem so basic that it doesn't even bear mentioning, but a surprising number of officers apparently don't think about it often enough. Obviously, there are times that an officer would prefer that his presence go unannounced in order to gain a tactical advantage. But it won't take a lot of noise to give away your position or announce your presence.

Walking, for example, is something that is done, for most people, with little thought or effort. However, when it is done in a tactical situation, such as a building search, it must be done with certain tactical considerations in mind. The first of these considerations is noise. You must practice walking quietly until you can do it as automatically as walking from the couch to the refrigerator. Then you must practice it some more, so that the skill is maintained. The shoes that you wear on duty must be chosen with tactics in mind. Different types of soles will affect your ability to walk quietly when necessary, as will different types of terrain. Once mastered, walking quietly will become a difficult habit to break. A sure sign of this is when those around you continually berate you for sneaking up on them, whether that was your intention or not.

The second consideration is balance. When involved in a tactical situation you cannot afford to trip and fall. A fall will undoubtedly make noise, and can very easily place you at a tactical disadvantage, especially in a situation where suspects have already been confronted, and are in close proximity. This too, makes it necessary to practice walking so that you can walk quietly while maintaining balance, even on a wide variety of terrains.

Again, it may sound simple, but it's these minor considerations that can add up and make the difference in a tactical situation. In fact, even all by itself, unnecessary noise can place you at a serious tactical disadvantage. The same is true of other tactical considerations. Individually, or together, they have the ability to make or break your tactics, and therefore must be taken seriously. Once you are aware of the tactical considerations involved in something as elementary as walking, you can then adapt tactically.

And what about movement? Can small movements make enough noise to cause tactical problems? The answer is, simply, "yes." Take duty belts and gear (holsters, handcuff cases, etc.) for example. In the past, all duty belts and gear were made of genuine leather, which tends to squeak when you walk or move around. The older the leather, the louder the squeak. Nowadays, although leather gear can still be purchased, many manufacturers make their products from various types of laminates, or nylon. Gear made from laminates or nylon is generally much quieter than leather, but you should still take notice of any noise made by these types of duty gear, and take whatever action is necessary to minimize it. Duty belts that utilize velcro to secure them to the under belt seem to be quieter than those that rely on belt keepers alone. The velcro system keeps the two belts tightly secured to each other so that they don't rub against one another, thus minimizing noise.

Patrol boots are also a consideration, not only in regard to the noise they make when you walk, but also the noise they can make when you are moving around. Many patrol boots are leather and can cause the same noise problems as leather duty belts. Nylon uppers seem to minimize the squeaky shoe syndrome and therefore might be a more tactical choice.

There are tactical considerations involved with other parts of the uniform, as well. The uniform jacket, for example, is not without its problems. A uniform jacket made of nylon will make noise when you move around, caused by the material rubbing against itself. A jacket made of a softer material will prove to be much quieter. A second consideration where jackets are concerned is the restriction of movement. A good uniform jacket must not be so restrictive that you do not have the full range of motion needed to do such things as defend yourself or others. Leather police jackets are probably among the worst of uniform jackets, where restriction of movement is concerned. They do, however, have some tactical advantages that they gain from their tough construction. They can offer limited protection when confronted with certain edged weapons, particularly those of the extremely dull variety. They are also, undoubtedly, invaluable for motorcycle officers.

Jackets must also be fitted and worn in such a way that they do not interfere with easy access to the equipment that you carry on your duty belt. The last thing you need in a stressful situation is to have to fumble for a piece of equipment that you need immediately. Accessing equipment quickly while wearing your duty jacket should be practiced, as the jacket can interfere to some degree, even when worn properly. Of course, it goes without saying that a duty jacket must keep you warm in addition to all these other considerations.

What other tactical considerations does the uniform hold? As I mentioned earlier, there will be times when you will prefer that your presence go unnoticed until you decide to announce yourself. But what else will give you away besides noise? Light, for one thing. Police uniforms have traditionally been a collection of brass buttons, nameplates, whistles, lanyards, and assorted other ornamentation. Not to mention the badge. These decorations, while very professional looking, can very easily give away your position by reflecting light. Moonlight, or a street light, reflecting off of a badge can be easily seen across a dark street. Of course, the amount of brass and nickel plated ornamentation that you wear on your uniform will probably not be left entirely up to you. There are certain parts of your uniform that will be required, and must be worn in order to conform to policy. The best that you can do to alleviate this concern is to avoid adding to the list of required items worn on your uniform, and to be aware of the potential problems that the required items may present. In the winter time you may have the option of covering up the excess reflective items with your uniform jacket, which will probably have fewer adornments than the uniform shirt. In warmer weather, however, this simply may not be an option.

And what about breathing? Is it really such a major consideration? If you expect to be able to search buildings, fields, or anything else without giving yourself away, it certainly deserves some thought. Breathing may seem to be such a quiet operation to begin with that it really can't get much quieter. It may also seem to be something that would be very easily controlled when necessary. Remember, though, that when it becomes necessary to control your breathing, it will not be under ordinary circumstances. Searching for a dangerous, or potentially dangerous, subject will most likely increase your heart rate and your breathing rate. In addition, it will often times be after pursuing a subject, or subjects, that a search begins. You may be involved in a struggle, followed by a foot pursuit, and then a search. Under these conditions, with the additional complication of a possible adrenalin rush to consider, your breathing will be rapid, heavy, and more difficult to control. This not only translates into a noise discipline problem, but can introduce other problems as well. For instance, think about how difficult it is to speak when you are out of breath. The words come out choppy and only with a great deal of effort. To make matters worse, this is one time when clear, intelligible speech is of the utmost importance. A subject confronted during a building search, no matter how cooperative he might be, will have a difficult time obeying your commands if he can't understand them. Additionally, communicating with other officers on the scene must be done in a clear and concise manner. So what can you do to curtail this problem? Obviously, the frequency and duration of the foot pursuits in which you will become involved will not be entirely in your control. Therefore, the problem must be approached from a different angle. The solution is simple. As a tactically minded officer, you must stay in shape. If you are in good physical condition, you will breathe easier after a foot pursuit, or a struggle. This will make it easier for you to control your breathing. And it follows that if you can control your breathing, you will be better able to speak under stress. Of course, the ability to speak more clearly while under stress is not the only reason to maintain a reasonable amount of physical fitness, but it's definitely a good one.

Another good reason to stay physically fit is the fact that physical skills and coordination can also be affected by such things as an increased heart rate. Even though it can be difficult to speak when under stress, think of how difficult it would be to point a weapon at a subject and keep it steady. This is a skill that could prove much more critical than issuing commands and should offer sufficient motivation for a continual physical fitness program. Of course, the most obvious and compelling reason to keep in good physical condition is the fact that fitness is crucial if you expect to be able to survive a violent physical attack.

Now let's take a look at how what you say can effect the outcome of a situation. Your voice is a tool that you have at your disposal and should be thought of that way. By using it properly you will be able to diffuse situations, calm people down, and often times you will be able to resolve potentially violent situations peacefully, and without using handcuffs. Conversely, by using your voice in the wrong way, you can add to an already hostile environment. You could escalate a situation, making an arrest, or worse, necessary when it otherwise would not have been. It is important to remember, however, that your voice is only one tool, to be used only when appropriate. It cannot, and should not, be counted on to diffuse all subjects or situations. Some people and some situations will always require stronger measures in order to handle them effectively. In these types of situations, your voice can be used as an *additional* tool in attempting to reach a peaceful resolve, so long as you are ready to take immediate action of some other form, should talking fail.

For example, suppose you are threatened by a subject armed with a knife. Imagine the subject is a fair distance away from you, and you have your weapon drawn and pointed at the subject, while you are positioned behind some type of cover as an obstacle that the subject must negotiate in order to attack. This might be an appropriate time to attempt to talk the subject into putting the knife down and giving up. You are in a position of advantage. You can afford to take the time to try to talk the subject down. If you are successful, you will have lost nothing more than time. If the subject does decide to attack, you will have sufficient time to react.

But if you have no cover, without your weapon drawn, and the subject is closing the distance with the knife raised in an apparent attack, it may not be an appropriate time for negotiations. Instead, your voice might best be used to give commands to the subject, ordering him to put the knife down, and warning him of the consequences if he fails to comply. And it's quite possible under these conditions, (depending on the distance of the subject, the speed of the attack, etc.) that using your voice might not be an option at all. You may not have the time to utter a single word before you are forced to take whatever action is necessary to stop the attack.

In situations where talking is the appropriate option, your use of verbal skills should be finely honed if it is to be effective. The first order of business is to obtain formal training in the use of verbal communications relating to law enforcement. Most basic police academies include instruction in this area. Of course it should not end there. You should seek out additional instruction whenever possible. This is another area of police work in which continual learning is an absolute necessity, and it will be available to you on a daily basis. You will continue to learn how to use your voice effectively, not only by attending formal training sessions, but also through the experience that you will gain in your dealings with the public. You will learn what to say, and what not to say, based on the circumstances, as you gain experience. It is all part of your awareness of yourself and your ability to influence people and affect your situation.

As for the awareness of your surroundings, its importance should be obvious. Police work can be very dangerous. But the dangers are not always immediately apparent. They can be caused by environmental conditions, emergency situations, or by the people that the job necessitates contact with. Whatever the cause, the danger is real, and the results can be just as disastrous if you are not cautious.

Environmental conditions can pose very high risks for officers. One of the most notable dangers in an officer's environment is traffic. Even though most of us were probably told by our mothers at a very early age not to play in the street, an officer's job puts him right in the middle of traffic on a regular basis. Whether directing traffic, investigating accidents, issuing citations, or pursuing a violator, the streets are a dangerous place. You will have to be alert to the danger presented by traffic, and have a genuine respect for it in order to stay safe. Many officers don't seem to take this danger seriously, but any officer who has been struck, or nearly struck, while out of the relative safety of the patrol vehicle takes it very seriously and always will. That is, if he survived. The same is true of officers that have survived high speed crashes.

The statistics change from year to year, but there is always a substantial number of officers that are accidentally killed in the line of duty (*Law Enforcement Officers Killed and Assaulted*). Many of these are killed in traffic related accidents. Some are killed when struck by vehicles and some during high speed pursuits. So what can be done to minimize this element of danger during your daily tour of duty? Traffic direction must be done from time to time, accidents must be investigated, and citations will probably always be a part of your patrol duties. So you will find yourself in the middle of streets, highways, and roads several times during each shift. The solution then is to be alert to the problem without being distracted by it. Because, while it is necessary to be alert to this particular danger, if you are distracted by it you could leave yourself open to an assault. As for pursuits, the same is true. You must be aware of the fact that your very life is in danger during high speed vehicle chases, regardless of your level of skill. Your survival attitude must carry over into pursuit driving, so that you will carefully weigh the violation that started the pursuit against the risks involved, and not take unnecessary chances with your life or the lives of the general public.

Additionally, there are numerous emergency situations that can pose dangers for officers. Officers are often times placed in situations on patrol that expose them to hazards such as fire, floods, downed power lines, and countless others. Again, the important thing is to not discount these hazards and remember that a downed power line can be as dangerous as any suspect with a gun.

Of course the most dangerous element in an officer's environment is man (and woman). The people that you will meet on a daily basis can be the most dangerous element in law enforcement. Men, women, and *children* have the ability to end your life. According to FBI statistics, offenders who kill law enforcement officers can be male or female and often times are under the age of eighteen.

Most people would never even think of doing such a thing, but some may actually attempt it. Whether or not they succeed depends largely on you. Your level of skill in overcoming an attack, and your attitude of survival will be crucial when faced with an actual attempt on your life. But in order for your skill and attitude to have their maximum effectiveness, you must be prepared for the attack. Therefore, alertness will have to play an important role in your survival attitude.

First, as discussed earlier, you must accept the fact that your life may at *any time* be placed in danger *by anyone* that you come into contact with. This means on duty or off, and regardless of assignment. Law enforcement officers have been assaulted during all types of duty assignments, not just on patrol. And perhaps because officers are usually more alert to what's happening around them all the time, they become involved in off duty encounters as well. It also means male or female, regardless of age. Officers have been assaulted by juveniles, and adults, ranging in age from the very young to the very old.

Secondly, to become a tactically minded officer you must understand, *and believe*, that it *can* happen. You certainly do not need to believe, however, that every person you encounter wishes to kill you. Such a belief could create a very paranoid and dangerous state of mind. But you do need to understand that people are not predictable, and while the number of people that would actually consider carrying out a violent assault on a peace officer is probably very low, you cannot predict which person, or persons, you meet may be thinking of doing something violent. You may encounter someone who is emotionally disturbed and does not possess the ability to determine rationally what is right or wrong. Or you may encounter a person that has no history of mental illness or violence, but has recently experienced a traumatic event in his or her life that has caused some very irrational thinking.

There are many different circumstances that could lead to an attack against an officer. The important thing to remember is that it *can* happen, at any time, under any set of circumstances. When you believe this, you will not be surprised by an attack when it does happen. A feeling of surprise, or disbelief, is not uncommon when officers are involved in violent encounters, such as gunfights. Some officers who have survived violent attacks have said afterwards that at first they could not believe that someone was shooting at them. This surprise, or disbelief, can cause hesitation on the part of the officer, and hesitation can be deadly. But if you believe that it can, and will, happen at some point during your career, you will not be surprised, or shocked, when it happens. Therefore, you will have less chance of hesitating and your response will be quicker. And, as you can imagine, a quick response will be critical in a life and death situation.

One way to avoid being caught off guard is to study and learn everything you can about body language, and then watch the people that you confront for danger signs in their movements. A person who is considering an attack will often give away his intentions by taking an aggressive stance or posture. A wide stance, clenched fists, or crossed arms are among the danger cues that you might see immediately before an attack.

Someone who is considering taking an officer's weapon will almost always look at the weapon before making a move. Remember that even an unarmed subject can have access to a weapon if you let him get too close to yours. And besides awareness that someone may try to take your weapon, you also have to be aware of any other weapons that may be available to the people that you confront on the job.

Even if you believe that someone is unarmed, they may have a weapon that doesn't immediately look like something dangerous. Disguised weapons can be made by innovative criminals, or even purchased at specialty stores, or through mail order catalogs. Knives can be disguised as lipsticks, belt buckles, pens, and other seemingly harmless objects. Firearms have been made from pagers, cigarette lighters, and even rolled up magazines.

And even if someone isn't carrying any obvious or disguised weapons, there may very well be ordinary objects in the nearby vicinity that would serve as adequate weapons. Depending on the environment, the person, or persons, that you are in contact with may have access to kitchen knives, scissors, screwdrivers, sticks, or any number of other potentially dangerous objects.

Being aware of your surroundings while dealing with people in a professional manner can be a fine line, and you will have to learn how to walk it carefully. While you are aware of the dangers in dealing with the public, and the fact that you must never let your guard down, you cannot approach everyone you come into contact with as if they are public enemy number one. Police work is, after all, public service and law enforcement officers are public servants.

So on top of everything else, now you must be able to stay alert to all of the potential dangers you may encounter, all the while remaining polite and professional in your dealings with the public. For example, when conducting a traffic stop, you have no way of knowing who you are dealing with. The person you stop may be the average, law abiding citizen who poses no threat to you other than possibly throwing a few insults in your direction under his breath. On the other hand, you may have stopped someone who poses a substantial threat to your safety. He may be someone having a bad day and looking for a fight. Or he may be intoxicated, or under the influence of drugs, and experiencing a violent reaction. Worse yet, he could be a wanted subject who will pose a substantial risk if he thinks that you know he is wanted and that your intent is to take him to jail.

The point is that you don't know who you are stopping or what his intentions are. Additionally, you don't know who you are dealing with when it comes to any passengers that might be in the stopped vehicle. Passengers can pose the same risks as the driver. They may not have anything to do with the reason you originally stopped the vehicle, but they may have something to hide all the same; which means that if they think you are about to take them to jail they can be just as dangerous as the driver. And since you don't know who you are dealing with, you have to be ready for anything. At the same time, you have to conduct yourself in a professional and courteous manner because statistically the majority of traffic stops turn out to be relatively uneventful.

Additionally, awareness includes being constantly cognizant of the whereabouts of your fellow patrol officers. In order to provide good backup for one another, you have to watch out for each other. This is an essential part of being a tactical thinker and a good law enforcement officer. Listen to the radio so that you know where everyone is. Check on each other whenever possible. Be sure that your fellow coworkers can depend on you to be there when they need you.

Once more, there is an awful lot to consider. But with patience, practice, and commitment you will be able to walk the fine line without a great degree of difficulty. You will be able to deal with citizens in a wide variety of situations requiring a vast range of responses. And you will be able to get through all of it without ever letting your guard down. And most people will never even know that the whole time you are in contact with them, you are prepared to handle any level of danger that may arise. All because you are aware and alert.

Remember the rule: Awareness, not paranoia.

"Courage is resistance to fear, mastery of fear - not absence of fear."
Mark Twain (1835-1910), U.S. author

3

Fear

If you ask several officers if they have ever known fear during the course of their duties, you can probably expect a wide variation in responses. Some may say that they have never been afraid. Others will readily admit to being scared to death on more than one occasion. Still others may "hem" and "haw" over the question and never really come up with a straight answer.

Why such a difference in responses? The most likely reason is the fact that police work has always been something of a "macho" career. Many peace officers are simply reluctant to admit that they are capable of being afraid. Of course, they are as capable of feeling fear as anyone else, whether they care to admit it or not. Yet, it seems that they are more in the minority nowadays, as the emotional side of law enforcement has become one of the most studied topics in law enforcement administration and training circles. Gone are the days when an officer would be ridiculed if he admitted to being afraid in a situation where anyone with an ounce of sense would be scared out of his mind.

Instead, today's officers will readily acknowledge that certain situations are likely to scare anyone. And it's okay for you to be afraid. The problem occurs when fear prevents you from doing your job. And if fear were to become such a controlling factor that you could not go about your assigned duties, patrolling your assigned area, without feeling afraid, you would definitely need to overcome this condition before you could expect to handle the job on a day-to-day basis.

But this is not the level of fear that you will probably be faced with. The situations in which most officers experience fear are those with a high level of apparent danger. It is in these situations that you will have to learn to master your fear, and remain in control. It's one thing to be scared while in the middle of a life and death situation, but it's another thing altogether to let that fear paralyze you or otherwise prevent you from doing the job that you need to do. In other words, you can expect to be afraid when faced with the possibility of death or bodily harm. There's absolutely no shame in it. It's your response to that fear that counts. And by expecting to be afraid, fear will not take you by surprise. You will be better able to control your fear if you are prepared for it.

So your level of fear in a given situation is not as important as the way you react to it. What then, should be your response to fear? The answer to this question depends on the situation and the level of fear. For example, when searching a building for an armed subject, you will probably experience a certain amount of fear. This is natural, and will subside to some degree as you gain experience in building searches. In fact, your first building search will possibly be one of the scariest of your career. Your response to this fear should be to continue with the task at hand, acknowledging your fear as a reminder that you are involved in a dangerous activity. Using fear in this manner can be a very effective tool in keeping you from exceeding your limitations and getting yourself in over your head. After all, that is what fear is for.

The first step in learning to control your fear, to the degree that it can be controlled, is to gain a basic understanding of what fear is, and why it is important. It is not necessary for you to become an expert on fear or to pursue a college degree on the subject, but it is helpful to understand that fear is designed as a defense mechanism in the human body, and that its purpose is to protect you from harm. In *Horror, Fright and Panic* fear is defined as "a reaction to a recognized threat that is characterized by an impulse to escape danger and a feeling of disagreeable tension."

When you experience fear, barring what is usually referred to as irrational fear, you experience it for a reason. The reasons vary and you have probably experienced fear in one form or another at some point in your lifetime. It may have been related to some traumatic event in your life, such as a car accident, or if you have been lucky, your worst experiences with fear have stemmed from relatively uneventful encounters with snakes or spiders or some other commonly feared creature. But regardless of the type of fear that you have experienced, or its cause, you have no doubt experienced the many physiological effects of fear. You have experienced a sudden increase in your heart rate; the feeling that your heart is pounding so strongly that it may burst out of your chest. You may have experienced the sudden onset of dry mouth. Or you may have experienced such things as goose pimples, or the hair on the back of your neck standing up. You may have even experienced what is commonly referred to as an adrenalin rush. All of these things are normal responses to the danger cues that you have perceived. Your body is reacting to these danger cues by preparing itself for the appropriate response to whatever danger you may be faced with.

The stronger, more rapid, heartbeat allows oxygen to be pumped more rapidly throughout your body. There is also a contraction of your spleen, releasing stored red blood cells to carry this additional oxygen. Your liver releases stored sugar for your muscles to use. The blood supply is efficiently redistributed from the skin and the viscera to the muscles and the brain. Breathing becomes deeper and the bronchi in the lungs become dilated so that more oxygen can be taken in. The pupils become dilated, possibly to increase visual efficiency. There is an increase in the special blood cells known as lymphocytes, which aid in the repair of damaged tissues. There is an increase in the blood's ability to coagulate, which helps to close wounds.

All of these things happen when the sympathetic nervous system works in conjunction with the hormones secreted by the adrenal medulla: epinephrine and nor epinephrine, also known as adrenalin and nor adrenalin. And it all happens within minutes, or even seconds. Some of these changes you will not even be aware of as they are happening; but as you can imagine, they are very important when you are in danger. All of these reactions by your body are designed to prepare you instantly for whatever response to danger is most appropriate in a given situation.

The two most instinctive responses are fight or flight. Most people who are faced with extreme danger will have one of these two impulses, which can be very strong. The instinct seems to be either to close in and eliminate the source of danger, or to escape it as quickly as possible. It is most likely an instinct that is as old as man himself. The two responses are very different, but each can be appropriate under certain conditions. For example, suppose while hiking in the woods you encounter a very large bear, accompanied by cubs. The mother bear's instinct may be one of fight rather than flight, as her interest is in protecting her young, and you may be perceived as a danger. Your most appropriate response if attacked by the mother bear would probably not be that of fight; because unless your name is Daniel Boone, you are no match for the bear and you probably have no desire to kill this bear who is defending her young anyway.

Now imagine that you are out for a walk with your small children, and you encounter a seemingly vicious dog. Like the mother bear, your interest will be in protecting your children. You know that you probably do not have the option of flight because you would have to carry the kids, and the dog may pursue you anyway. Your most appropriate response, then, will possibly be that of fight. Of course, the "fight" might simply entail an aggressive move in the dog's direction, or some other action intended to trigger the dog's flight reaction; but it is all part of the fight response.

A third instinctive response to sudden fear is to freeze. This is actually a passive form of the flight response, and although it may be appropriate in the situation involving the mother bear (playing dead), there are probably not very many other situations you will encounter that will call for this response. And it is undoubtedly useless in police work. As a police officer you will be expected to handle any and all situations you are faced with in the course of your duties. And while the flight response could become necessary under extreme conditions, to simply freeze up when faced with danger could by no means be interpreted as handling the situation. In fact, even the flight response would probably be appropriate only under the most extreme conditions, and then it must be only a temporary flight in order to gain some kind of tactical advantage before re-engaging. And even that could not be justified unless you are all by yourself, or all of the officers involved take the same option of disengagement together. You cannot afford to leave anyone behind.

Because you will be the police officer who is called to the scene to resolve the situation, you must learn how to control your "fight or flight" instincts. Law enforcement officers are the ones who are always seen running in the direction of the gunshots while everyone else is screaming and running away. It just doesn't seem quite right, does it? But when the public is placed in danger, by whatever means, someone must be willing to confront the situation head-on in order to protect innocent lives. And you will be able to do this by controlling your fight or flight response.

This will come about through training, experience, and preparation. You already know that you, as an officer, cannot afford to let your fight or flight (or freeze) instincts control you when faced with danger on the job. But should these instincts be ignored? No, of course not. Like any other instinct, you must learn to trust them to some degree. Remember that you have had these instincts for a long time, but you are just now venturing into police work. In the beginning of your career, there may be somewhat of an imbalance between your initial instincts and what is an appropriate response based on your training and your skills. For example, in the early stages of your career, if confronted with a dangerous situation, your first instinct may be flight. But because you are well trained, and prepared to handle the situation, this will probably not be the most appropriate response. You will, instead, control that instinct, take charge of the situation, and do your job. In time, with experience, your instincts and your abilities will begin to balance out, so that your instincts become even more trustworthy, and deserve more consideration. But they should never be totally ignored. Your instincts serve a very important function.

Fear is one of these all-important instincts. It is designed to alert you to imminent danger so that you can take whatever steps are necessary to protect yourself. The steps that you take will naturally depend on the circumstances. For the most part, the fear that you experience will cause you only to be more alert to the danger that you face. In some cases the fear will be sufficient to cause you to examine why you are in the situation that you are in, and consider ways to get out of it. This is how you will be tested: not only in how you respond to fear on your most instinctive level, but in your abilities to make tactical decisions, as well.

In other words, there are some situations in which fear should only serve to keep you on your toes while you continue to take care of business. These are the situations that you will encounter most often. Additionally, you will find yourself faced with situations that require you to seriously consider the option of backing off and waiting for additional assistance before proceeding any further. When and under what circumstances you determine that you need to wait for help before continuing will be up to you. You will have to decide for yourself, based on your level of training and experience, when it is reasonably safe to proceed alone and when you should wait for backup. Remember, aside from compliance with departmental policies, this is *your* decision. You are the only one who must be comfortable with your decisions in this area. If you think you need to wait for backup, wait for backup. If you think you can handle the situation by yourself, then by all means proceed.

Of course, the responsibility for the results of the decision that you make will be yours, and yours alone. If you make the wrong decision, you will have to accept the consequences. If you are wrong in deciding to wait for backup, the suspects may be able to escape or continue their criminal activities while you are waiting. And you will have to live with the results of the extra time that you allowed them to have while waiting to proceed. On the other hand, if you proceed on your own when it's not really safe to do so, you could needlessly endanger your life. Clearly, based on this, it would be better for your own safety to err on the side of waiting for backup, rather than rushing in prematurely.

All in all, your decisions will be based on your training, experience, and your level of skill, not on your level of fear. You will learn your limitations as you gain experience and this will serve to guide you as you find yourself in difficult situations. Again, fear must serve only as an alert system, warning you of the dangers ahead. You cannot allow it to be a controlling factor as you go about your duties. Conversely, the value of fear cannot be discounted. Without fear, you could very easily get yourself into a situation that you cannot get out of.

When you do experience fear, acknowledge it; but don't focus on it. If you focus on the level of danger that is present, and the resulting fear, you may feel vulnerable and weak. But if you focus on your strengths and your abilities, you will feel confident and in control of the situation. And taking control of the situation is your job.

"Authority is not a quality one person 'has,' in the sense that he has property or physical qualities. Authority refers to an interpersonal relation in which one person looks upon another as somebody superior to him."
Erich Fromm (1900-1980), U.S. psychologist

4

Command Presence

When you arrive at a scene, everyone involved will know immediately that you are in charge. And not because you are a law enforcement officer, in uniform, wearing a badge and carrying a gun. In fact, to many people, these things will be irrelevant. Nevertheless, it will be clear that you have arrived and that you intend to take control of the situation. It will be clear that you are in charge because of the way you present yourself, from the moment you arrive on scene. This is what is known as command presence.

If you believe that everyone you encounter on the job will be sufficiently influenced by the fact that you are an officer, and that they will be compliant simply because you are the law, you will soon learn the error in this line of thinking. This is a common misconception among those new to law enforcement; and even though it is usually disproved after just a short period of time on the job, it will be helpful if you can avoid this period of adjustment altogether. Of course, there is a certain percentage of people in society who have the utmost respect for the law, and will always be respectful and compliant when you deal with them. The problem is these are not the people you will be dealing with most often. At least not in the type of situations in which immediate control is necessary. You will most likely meet these people in situations where tempers are not running very high, and the atmosphere is fairly calm, such as during report calls. Their respectful, compliant attitude will be apparent immediately, regardless of whether they are the victim of crime and they require your assistance, or because they are genuinely respectful of peace officers.

Most situations you will be required to quickly gain control of, will be those of a more urgent nature, such as domestic violence calls or bar fights. And in these situations, tempers will be flaring, emotions will be running high; and just to make things interesting, there will probably be drugs or alcohol involved. This is where you will find those people who are not impressed with your shiny badge, your freshly pressed uniform, or the modest arsenal you carry on your duty belt. And so the way that you present yourself when you first arrive will be critical.

You must instantly convey an image of professionalism and authority that will cause even the most high spirited people at the scene to think twice before getting in your way. This isn't always easy, especially when you consider that some people will always require stronger measures to control them, no matter how good your command presence is. You must project to everyone at the scene that you are in complete control of the situation, and that you cannot be intimidated. This is not to be confused with cockiness or a "badge heavy" attitude. Like other areas of law enforcement, there is a fine line to walk here, also. You must be able to convey confidence without appearing cocky, or arrogant. If you cross over the line, you will achieve the opposite of the desired goal. Instead of gaining compliance, you will provoke antagonism. And then you will have gained nothing.

So how do you walk this line successfully? Command presence starts with your appearance. The way that you wear your uniform and the way that you carry yourself are two basic elements in developing good command presence. If you do not maintain your uniform properly you cannot possibly hope to portray a professional image. And your supervisors will not be the only ones to take notice of this. The people you deal with on patrol will interpret this as a lack of professionalism, and quite possibly they will equate it with incompetence. First impressions *are* important.

Imagine that you are eating dinner, when suddenly you become violently ill. You are rushed to the hospital and taken to an examination room. After a short time a man dressed in rags, who appears to be someone who has just wandered in from the street, enters the examination room and begins to conduct the exam, identifying himself as the doctor on call. You would most likely, and quite understandably, be a little bit apprehensive about this doctor's credentials, *at least initially.* As it turns out, he *is* the doctor -- he was attending a costume party when he was paged by the hospital, so he didn't take the time to change clothes before returning to the hospital. After the initial apprehension of being examined by a hobo wears off, you will draw your own conclusions about what kind of a doctor you are dealing with. You will base these conclusions on his demeanor, and your overall impression of him, not on his appearance. After all, he could be the best or the worst doctor in the hospital, or anywhere in between. The fact that he happened to be attending a costume party when you became ill has nothing to do with his competence or incompetence as a medical professional.

But just as you would have second thoughts about seeing a doctor who enters the examination room dressed inappropriately, the people you meet will form opinions about what kind of an officer you are based on your appearance, *at least initially.* If you show up at a scene looking professional, you may initially be perceived as a professional. This initial impression will help you to continue to portray a professional image and may therefore be helpful in gaining compliance. Conversely, if you do not make a professional first impression, you will have to work that much harder to convince those people you encounter that you are a capable professional. Now you will have to work to change their opinion of you, which they formed when you first arrived. It is much easier to make a good impression in the first place.

Because it is true that some people will not be impressed by the sharpness of the creases in your uniform or the spit shine on your boots, you must not be dependent on your uniform's appearance alone to project command presence. If a professional looking uniform were all that is necessary to gain compliance, anyone with a steam iron and a can of shoe polish could be an officer. But it doesn't work that way. Your uniform is only part of the equation. It *assists* you in portraying a professional attitude.

Take pride in your uniform and take good care of it. Keep it well pressed and properly creased. Keep loose threads trimmed. Replace patches as they get old even if the shirt is still serviceable. Keep your shoes polished as best you can. This will not always be easy depending on the working environment of your particular assignment. If you spend a lot of time patrolling dirt roads, for example, you may be fighting a losing battle by trying to keep a spit shine on your boots everyday. And don't forget about buttons and brass on your uniform. Remember to polish your name plate, badge, and any other uniform ornamentation you may wear. Replace these items when necessary.

Your duty gear also plays a part in your overall professional image. Your duty belt and all the gear attached to it should be regularly maintained with whatever cleaning or polishing products that the manufacturer recommends, depending on whether your gear is made of leather or a laminate. And while you're at it, this is also a good time to inspect all of your gear for wear and tear. Weakened duty gear should be replaced immediately, to decrease the possibility of your sidearm, or another piece of your equipment, being taken away from you during an altercation, or lost during a foot chase.

But remember, the uniform is only part of the initial impression that you make when you enter a room. The way you carry yourself is also very important in command presence. A professional attitude is your goal. Suppose for example that you are on your meal break when you are called away to a domestic dispute. You leave your meal to get cold and respond to the call for service. When you arrive, tempers are flaring, but there has been no violence to speak of yet. You know you must take control of the situation in order to keep it from escalating. This is important for the safety of everyone involved. If you come across as genuinely concerned about the welfare of those involved, you will probably get more compliance than if you were to portray an attitude of boredom or apathy, or otherwise let it be known that you are not happy about missing your lunch.

And remember that regardless of who called you to the domestic dispute, there is probably at least one participant who does not want you there. Let them know why you are there, and try to assure them that you are not there to interfere, as they may very well accuse you of. You are there because you were called to the scene, and now you have a duty to ensure that everything is okay before you can leave. And if anyone there has broken the law, your duty is to arrest them and charge them appropriately. You don't have to go into this much detail; just let them know you are there for a reason and the sooner they cooperate with you, the sooner you can be on your way, and out of their way.

It's difficult to describe professionalism and command presence, but the important thing to remember is that the people you deal with will be very cognizant of how you present yourself. If you show genuine concern for their well being, they will sense this immediately. If you come across as cocky or overconfident, you may very well be challenged. And if you appear unprofessional, or incompetent, you may be at a greater risk of attack by someone who is considering taking you down.

Take traffic stops for example. When you stop a vehicle for a traffic infraction, such as speeding or running a red light, you don't know who you are dealing with. You may have stopped an ordinary, law abiding citizen, or you may be about to confront an armed and dangerous felon. Since you don't know which it is, you will be very cautious and use the proper tactics for this type of vehicle stop. Now suppose that you *have* stopped an armed and dangerous subject. He is very agitated at being stopped by you, and he is well aware of the fact that he is wanted. He also knows that if you are aware that he is wanted, or if you find out, he will soon be back in prison. He then begins to consider using his weapon against you in order to make good his escape. But as you exit your vehicle, and as you make your approach, he begins to think twice about taking you on. Why? Because he can tell by watching you that you know what you are doing. He notices your professional appearance as you get out of the patrol car. He notices the way you approach; cautiously, yet confidently. He notices your professional attitude in talking to him. You are business like, without talking down to him. He puts all these things together and decides that you are well prepared to defend yourself should you have to. He knows that in order for his attack on you to be successful, he needs the element of surprise on his side. And because he sees you as a well trained professional, he isn't sure that he can take you by surprise. He also begins to take into account your abilities and the level of skill that you most likely possess based on your professional demeanor. And even though he doesn't want to go back to prison, he wants even less to be shot and killed, which is exactly what he thinks will happen if he tangles with a well trained, well prepared officer. So he just might change his mind about launching an attack. All because of the way that you presented yourself from the beginning.

It probably wouldn't be the first time that a violent assault has been averted because of good command presence. The problem is that we don't usually find out when someone was considering a violent assault on an officer, and then decided against it at the last minute, regardless of the reasons. Chances are that most officers have come close to being assaulted many more times than they will ever know about. But when the potential assailant changes his mind, the officer goes about his business, never knowing that the person he was dealing with was contemplating an assault. The assault that they were contemplating may not have been anything as violent as a shooting, or a stabbing, but an assault nonetheless.

We do, however, hear about the reasons that bad guys decide to kill officers. And many times the officer's level of command presence plays a part. Law enforcement officers have been killed because they were perceived as careless or unprepared by their assailants. According to studies published in *Killed in the Line of Duty*, it was not uncommon for offenders who kill law enforcement officers to evaluate the officers prior to committing to an assault. In one such case study an offender who had set out to kill an officer aborted an attack on the first officer he encountered after evaluating that officer. He then launched a successful attack on the next officer that he encountered after deciding that the second officer would be an easy target.

One subject involved in a similar case study, also published in *Killed in the Line of Duty*, stated that the officer that he killed "was not authoritarian and did not take control of me. He was a willing participant in his death." Other offenders stated that they felt that if the officers that were killed had been more "professional" they would not have been killed.

Based on this information, you should find it very difficult to discount the importance of command presence.

"The basic tool for the manipulation of reality is the manipulation of words. If you can control the meaning of words, you can control the people who must use the words."
Philip K. Dick (1928-82), U.S. science fiction writer

5

Tactical Terminology

What in the world is tactical terminology? Simply put, what I call tactical terminology is any term used to describe a particular area of law enforcement as accurately as possible, in order to instill the proper attitude. Its importance lies in the fact that the words used to describe something can affect your attitude toward it.

If, for example, I were to tell you that in the course of your duties as a law enforcement officer you would be conducting routine traffic stops, you would probably not picture yourself using your patrol vehicle for cover, exchanging gunfire with the occupants of the stopped vehicle. And you probably wouldn't picture yourself being bounced off the hood of a vehicle that struck you as it passed by your routine stop. You wouldn't picture these things because I used the word "routine" in describing the vehicle stop, and these things are anything but routine.

Yet these things happen on traffic stops all too frequently. Why then, would anyone refer to traffic stops as routine? Almost no one does anymore. You will probably not hear the term used by anyone in law enforcement, especially law enforcement trainers. It is still used in the media quite often, especially when something newsworthy develops from a "routine traffic stop."

But the term is simply not tactical. It implies that you are involved in an activity that poses little or no risk of physical injury. By doing so, it can lull you into a false sense of security. You would then be at an increased risk of injury, because if you are dealing with a potentially violent individual, you will not be prepared for a confrontation as you will have let your guard down. You must remember that while not everyone you stop will be a violent fugitive from justice, nothing is routine; and nothing should be referred to as such.

The idea that your attitude and your approach to a situation can be affected by the term used to describe that situation is not new. Alfred Korzybski, a Polish-born American semanticist, first gave us the principle he referred to as "general semantics" in 1933, in a book entitled *Science and Sanity: An Introduction to Non-Aristotelian Systems and General Semantics*. Korzybski believed that words and behavior are interrelated, and that human behavioral responses can be improved through a more critical use of words. Ever since then, semanticists have been studying the relationship between words and behavior, using Korzybski's doctrine as the basis for their studies. It's not necessary for you to become a student of the Korzybski doctrine, or to become an expert in the field of general semantics in order to be a tactical thinker. But you should understand that a relationship between words and actions does exist, and that words can have a distinct positive or negative effect on the way you approach your patrol duties.

First, let's take a look at an example of how words can affect us. If you're like many people, when you hear the sound of fingernails on a chalkboard, you may start to shudder or shiver. In fact, it's quite possible that you have experienced the very same reaction anytime someone even mentions the idea of fingernails on a chalkboard, or perhaps you shuddered just now as you read the words. This is just one example of how words can cause reactions within us on more than one level.

Another example comes from a study cited in *Eye Witness Testimony: Civil and Criminal.* In this study test subjects watched a simulated motor vehicle accident on film. When asked later about what they had seen, the responses changed according to the wording of the question. Those who were asked, "How fast were the cars going when they smashed into each other?" gave higher speed estimates than those who were asked, "How fast were the cars going when they hit each other?" Changing just one word in the question led to higher estimates of speed, even though all participants watched the same film. This, again, illustrates how words can effect us, many times without our knowledge.

Now, let's examine a few of the different terms, both tactical and non-tactical, that you will hear during your training. Let's begin with vehicle stops, of which there are two basic kinds. The first type is a vehicle stop for a nonviolent offense such as a traffic violation. This is the type of vehicle stop that the media refers to as a routine traffic stop. The second is a vehicle stop involving a situation where you have information that the subjects you are stopping have, or may have, committed a serious crime and may be armed and dangerous. An example of this type of stop would be the stopping of a vehicle and subjects that match the description of a vehicle and subjects involved in an armed robbery.

Beginning with the first type, many officers have been taught to regard this as a low risk stop. Of course, if you consider the fact that law enforcement officers are killed or injured during these vehicle stops every year, the level of risk could hardly be considered low. Regardless of the statistics, the fact that the potential exists for you to be killed during these vehicle stops is an indicator that you need to be cognizant of the danger involved. Therefore the use of the term low risk is not much better than the use of the word "routine." The only reason it could be considered better at all is the fact that it does imply a certain amount of risk. But it does not accurately convey the level of risk you will be facing when conducting a traffic stop. And if it does not do this, it cannot be considered a tactical term. If you think of traffic stops as "low risk," you may become complacent or lazy in your use of tactics. Your chances of survival will then be based on luck rather than skill and attitude.

It would be much more tactical to use the term "unknown risk" to describe the same type of vehicle stop. This term will help you to develop the proper attitude necessary for conducting traffic stops safely. By thinking of traffic stops as unknown risk stops, you will be acknowledging the fact that every traffic stop contains a certain amount of risk, which can range from low to high. And since you won't know the exact level of risk you are dealing with, you will have to use tactics that allow for an immediate response to any threat that may present itself during the course of the stop. If all goes well, and you eventually send the violator on his way, you will have lost nothing. You will neither have wasted tactics nor have been overly cautious. You will have simply been prepared for the worst. This will prove to be very valuable if the vehicle stop goes bad. It also helps you to develop and maintain the proper tactics and the proper mindset for use on all of your future traffic stops.

If you approach all traffic stops of this type as unknown risk stops, the proper tactics will become habit. This, in turn, will increase your chances of surviving a violent encounter. It will also cause you to be more likely to continually reassess the level of risk that you are dealing with during traffic stops. You will be more alert to changes in the level of risk that may require you to make adjustments in your tactics. And, if you believe that any traffic stop can go bad, you will be mentally prepared, and not taken by surprise if you are assaulted. If you are caught off guard, your reaction time could suffer. And the loss of even one second in a gunfight can be very costly.

The other type of vehicle stop is one in which you have reason to believe that you may be dealing with armed and dangerous subjects, and is known in tactical terms as a "high risk" stop. It is commonly, though less tactically, referred to as a "felony stop." The term "high risk stop" is a very tactical term in that it accurately conveys the potential for danger that you face. It leaves you with almost no choice but to consider the stop a potentially life-threatening encounter and to select your tactics accordingly. You will learn the appropriate tactics for this type of stop during your basic training.

When you begin areas of training that involve physical skills, such as defensive tactics, or firearms training, you will begin to hear a variety of terms used to differentiate between your right and left sides. Some of the more common terms used are the terms "weak hand" and "weak side," or "strong hand" and "strong side." These terms do, however, seem to be disappearing from training as more tactical terms are taking over. To use the word "weak" in training has negative connotations. It implies a weakness that you may not be able to overcome. The focus is not on your ability to use either hand well, but on the fact that one hand may not be as effective as the other, to the point of being ineffective. It may be true that if you are right-handed, you may not be able to use your left hand as effectively as your right, especially if you don't train equally with both hands. But you will be behind the power curve if you believe that one hand is weak. This belief can be especially damaging if you are injured in an attack and you're left with only one hand to neutralize your attacker.

When you begin firearms training, you may hear the term "support hand." This term is more tactical because it has less negative connotations. It does, however, lack positive connotations. It implies that the sole purpose of the hand is support; that without the strong hand it is useless. Still, it is preferable to the term "weak hand." And even the terms "strong side" and "strong hand" have some tactical problems.

They may seem tactical at first glance, but to say that one is strong is to say that the other is weak.

The terms that are used in the medical profession, **dominant** and **non-dominant** have recently made an appearance in training circles; and you may hear them during your training. These terms are more tactical because they have no implications whatsoever regarding the abilities of either hand. They simply acknowledge the fact that one hand is used more frequently than the other in performing certain tasks.

The term used to describe tactical training should be tactical as well. You may hear either the term ''Officer Survival'' or the term ''Officer Safety.'' The term ''Officer Safety'' appears to be slowly taking over as the term ''Officer Survival'' is used less and less in academy training. This may be due to the fact that it is more ''politically correct.'' It is a ''softer'' term that sounds less aggressive and less intimidating, and in today's world of community policing softer terms are much more readily accepted.

It is not, however, tactical. ''Officer Safety'' is a term that brings to mind such things as wearing your orange vest while directing traffic, or wearing your seat belt while driving. Of course, these precautions are important for safety; and it follows that to survive, you must be safe. The idea, however, is to use terms that will accurately convey to you the fact that your physical survival is at stake. The term ''Officer Survival'' does this quite well by being ''tactically correct'' rather than ''politically correct.'' If you are trained in survival, as opposed to safety, you may as a result be more tactically minded. You will then be better prepared to handle a violent encounter, because you are thinking tactically. And by using proper tactics, you may be able to diffuse a situation before it has a chance to become violent.

In working toward developing a survival attitude, part of the process must include a concerted effort to maintain your survival attitude and your ability to think tactically, throughout your entire career. The terminology used during basic training can play a large part in how successful you are at this. The terms that you learn in the academy will stay with you for life. If you are taught in the academy that stopping a vehicle for speeding is considered a "low risk" stop, you will have difficulty thinking of this type of traffic stop in any other way. Likewise, if you are taught from the start to use tactical terminology, you will have equal difficulty considering any traffic stop to be "low risk." As a result, this may help you to live longer.

"The imagination is man's power over nature."
Wallace Stevens (1879-1955), U.S. poet

6

Mental Rehearsal

By now you know the importance of practice in becoming a survival oriented officer. You understand that you must work to maintain both your physical survival skills and your survival attitude. Mental rehearsal is one tool that you can use to help accomplish this. Mental rehearsal is just what it sounds like. It is practicing a skill or task, using the power of your mind and your imagination. It can help to increase your level of confidence in your skills and can actually help to improve your abilities.

The concept of mental rehearsal, or mental practice, has been around since the early 1940's, but the general idea has been studied as early as 1892 when Dr. Joseph Jastrow began research that is considered to be the beginning of scientific interest between the mental process and physical skills.

There have since been many studies done concerning the benefits of mental rehearsal. The studies were done using a variety of skills, test subjects and methods. Some studies involved physical tasks or athletic abilities while others involved mental challenges. The test methods have included mental rehearsal alone, practice alone, and a combination of the two. The results of the many different studies vary somewhat, as do the opinions of the different researchers, but all in all, mental rehearsal appears to have received favorable results. Researchers have not discounted the benefits of mental rehearsal. In *The Nature and Conditions of Learning*, Howard L. Kingsley wrote "the development of skill requires physical practice on the part of the learner, although mental practice can assist the process.''

Mental rehearsal can be very beneficial for you, the officer. It can be used to help maintain your physical survival skills, as well as your survival attitude. First, let's look at how it can assist you in the upkeep of your physical skills. The first and foremost rule to remember when using mental rehearsal is that it is not a substitute for practice. It should be used in conjunction with practice, and it can augment practice, but it is not a substitute for practice.

Let's use the example of defensive tactics training. When you learn defensive tactics, or hand-to-hand defense during your academy training, you will most likely learn a substantial number of techniques in a relatively short amount of time. This is just the nature of the business. Trainers have a limited amount of time in an academy setting to provide you with the best possible training that they can. It is easy to see how the skills you develop during this training could deteriorate very rapidly if not maintained.

So, naturally, you must practice. This is one of those areas of training that spouses typically become involved in, usually as unwitting, or unwilling, defensive tactics partners. Recruits attending the academy always seem to enjoy returning home to demonstrate a wrist lock, or an arm bar takedown, on the first available volunteer. If you choose to practice all the great stuff you learn in the academy, using your spouse as the subject, be sure that your partner is both willing and able to handle the techniques that you plan to practice. And be careful not to hurt your partner. Your spouse will have enough to deal with while you're in the academy without being subjected to physical injury.

Ideally, practice should be done with other trained officers, under the supervision of a trained instructor. This is not always possible, or practical, and you must work with the resources that are available to you. Whatever the extent of your training and practice, mental rehearsal can play an important role. During practice sessions, it can be helpful to visualize yourself performing the required technique, with the desired result, before actually doing it hands on. This, as I mentioned earlier, can help to improve your skills and your confidence level.

In order for mental rehearsal to work with this type of training, you first have to know how to do the technique properly. This is important because if you don't know how to perform a technique properly, you won't be able to visualize it properly. And if you don't visualize yourself performing the technique properly, you will be defeating the purpose of mental rehearsal. It only works when you visualize yourself performing each individual technique properly, from start to finish.

So the first step is to learn proper defensive tactics techniques. Next, you must practice your hand-to-hand skills on a regular basis. And lastly, you should incorporate mental rehearsal of these skills into your training sessions. In addition, you can utilize mental rehearsal to improve your skills aside from practice sessions. Again, while it is important to remember that mental rehearsal is not a substitute for practice, there is no reason why it can't be beneficial outside of a training environment.

You will most likely have a limited amount of time available in your schedule for practice, and everyone needs to take time to relax now and then. But there will be times when you may not be able to do hands-on practice for one reason or another. You may not have anyone to practice with. Or perhaps you just don't have the time to practice. But you may have the time to simply visualize the techniques that you wish to practice. It only takes a few minutes. If you spend just a few minutes in mental rehearsal, you can gain some of the same benefits that you would realize in actual practice. By doing mental rehearsal, you will keep the techniques, along with their proper application, fresh in your mind.

And mental rehearsal is easy. It can be done almost anywhere, and at almost any time. Simply take a few minutes and pick a particular technique or skill and visualize yourself performing it properly. Then do it again. And again. You get the idea. Then try changing things up a bit. Don't change the technique yet, but try changing the subject that you are up against in your mind's eye. Use the same technique against a larger individual than you were picturing originally. Picture yourself overcoming different levels of resistance; from minimal resistance all the way up to extreme aggression. Imagine yourself making adjustments in the technique for those unexpected details that seldom appear in a training environment, such as large, bulky clothing that can make handcuffing more difficult. Then use your imagination and create some variations of your own.

After that, you may want to try changing the technique that you are mentally rehearsing. Go through the same variations in the scenario with different techniques. You may even want to try visualizing having difficulty with the subject while using one technique, and then mentally switching to another technique, which is successful in your scenario. Because, as you know, not all defensive tactics techniques will work on all people, and sometimes you have to be ready to switch to a different technique, if your first choice fails. Just remember that whatever variations you introduce into your mental rehearsal, you should always visualize yourself winning in the end. Otherwise, you will be defeating the purpose of mental rehearsal by setting yourself up to fail.

Now let's look at how you can use mental rehearsal to help you to maintain your survival attitude. The way to do this is to visualize yourself in many different situations involving tactical decisions and various levels of risk. You can imagine yourself confronted with a subject armed with a gun, or several subjects armed with guns. You can picture yourself up against a knife-wielding assailant, or up against multiple unarmed assailants.

You can imagine that you're responding to an armed robbery in progress, or that you're involved in a high speed pursuit. The possibilities are endless. They are limited only by your imagination.

This type of mental rehearsal should also be changed around and varied as much as possible. For example, suppose you were doing mental rehearsal using an armed robbery as the basis for your scenario. You might want to start with a situation involving one suspect armed with a knife, robbing a convenience store late at night with no one around but the clerk. Then when you have completed that scenario, you might change the weapon from a knife to a gun. Next, you might add a customer to the scenario, or perhaps add a second suspect. You might try a scenario that has the suspect, or suspects, inside the store when you arrive, and then change it to outside.

As you can see there are many possibilities for a robbery scenario alone. When you add in all the other types of calls that you will respond to, you end up with a never ending source of mental rehearsal material. Seemingly endless variations of scenarios can be created for domestic disturbances, burglaries, fight calls, traffic stops, foot pursuits and vehicle pursuits, just to name a few. The list goes on and on.

Again, mental rehearsal can be done almost anywhere, and at any time. The time that many officers utilize for this is the down time that often occurs on patrol. This is really one of the best times to do mental rehearsal because you can actually see the layout of your scenario. Just be sure you don't allow yourself to become so involved in your mental rehearsal that you forget to pay attention to your surroundings. Now, suppose you are on patrol on a slow night. As you drive by one of the local convenience stores in your patrol area, you can ask yourself, "What would I do if I saw an armed subject robbing that store right now?" And, viola, a scenario is born. Now you have an actual layout for your scenario. You can utilize the scene exactly as it is. The actual number of customers in the store will be in your scenario, along with the actual number of vehicles in the parking lot. You will have to deal with these things in your mental rehearsal just as you would in an actual tactical situation. You can use the vehicles, or other objects in the scene as cover, as you visualize yourself responding to the scene.

The scene will also be dynamic, so you can make adjustments in your tactical plan as the layout changes. New customers will arrive to pick up a few items, just as they would if an actual robbery were taking place. And you will have to decide how to handle them as they unknowingly put themselves in harm's way.

Just as in the defensive tactics scenarios we discussed earlier, the most important thing to remember is to always visualize yourself winning at the end of each scenario in your mental rehearsal. Of course, this doesn't mean that you should imagine yourself swooping down from the sky like a super hero, catching bullets in your teeth and saving the day just in the nick of time. It only means that you shouldn't visualize yourself being killed by the suspects. To do so would create the opposite of the mindset that you are trying to develop.

It can be beneficial, however, to imagine yourself getting injured, and continuing to get the job done, in your scenario. Part of mental rehearsal is training yourself never to give up, even if you are shot, or stabbed, or injured in some other way. So, it may help you to develop this mindset if you imagine that you could become injured, and then imagine yourself fighting through the pain and coming out of the situation victorious.

I wouldn't, however, recommend that your injury in your scenario be the result of an imaginary tactical error on your part. This would also be self-defeating. It would be better to imagine that if you are injured, it was simply the result of incredible luck on the part of the suspect. And the majority of the scenarios that you play out when mentally rehearsing, should not even include any injuries to you. Scenarios in which you are injured should only be done once in a while to reinforce your attitude of being able to survive under any circumstances.

However you use mental rehearsal, use it often. It can help you to prepare for all kinds of tactical situations and critical incidents. It can help you make the appropriate tactical decisions and keep your skills sharp for these situations.

"Perhaps life is just that ... a dream and a fear."
Joseph Conrad (1857-1924), Polish-born English novelist

7

Effects of Sudden Stress

There are other effects of sudden stress, or sudden fear, that you may experience during a critical incident that you should be aware of. Like the other effects of fear I mentioned earlier, you will be better able to handle these things if you are prepared for them to happen to you, long before they actually come your way. These additional results of fear and stress are such things as tunnel vision or auditory exclusion, for example, and can have an effect on the way you perceive events at times of high stress, as well as your ability to perform under stressful conditions.

When you experience something like tunnel vision, the first thing that will be effected is your ability to respond to the situation. Of course, it won't totally destroy your level of effectiveness, but it can have a negative impact. Imagine if you will, that you are conducting a traffic stop, when you are suddenly confronted with a life or death decision. The driver of the vehicle gets out of the car and points a gun at you. Suddenly you find yourself totally fixated on the weapon in the driver's hand. Everything surrounding the gun appears fuzzy and out of focus, and may even seem to disappear from view entirely. Yet, the gun is in very sharp focus. In fact, it may seem so clear you would swear you could read the serial number if the gun were simply turned in the right direction. This is tunnel vision, and although it probably won't prove to be very detrimental to your ability to neutralize the threat from the driver, it may leave you entirely vulnerable to an attack from another direction. If a passenger in the vehicle decides to join the assault, you may be so focused on the initial threat that you fail to notice you are under attack from two sides. The disadvantages here are obvious.

As for affecting your perception of events, it is easy to see how this can happen. And the disadvantages of a distorted perception should also be obvious. Aside from the tactical considerations that I just mentioned, you also have to take into account the effect on your ability to accurately recount the details of what has transpired, when it's time to write your report, or give a statement to investigators. Based on all of this, it should be easy to see how things such as tunnel vision can affect you during and after a critical incident.

Now let's take a more in depth look at some of the effects of extreme stress that you may have to deal with, and the ways they can affect your performance under fire. We'll continue with tunnel vision. As I mentioned, tunnel vision is very much like its name suggests. Your eyes become extremely focused on one area of concern and everything around it becomes either blurry or black. The main tactical disadvantage to tunnel vision, as I mentioned earlier, is that you can become overly focused on an initial threat, and leave yourself vulnerable to another assault from elsewhere. Another disadvantage to consider is that if you get tunnel vision when faced with a gun and you make the decision to shoot, you may not place your shots as accurately as you would otherwise. If you tunnel in on the gun, your shots will probably be directed at the gun. It's not uncommon for arms, hands, and guns to be shot during gunfights, because officers and their assailants are equally susceptible to tunnel vision.

Tunnel vision is a physiological response to high stress or sudden fear, and it is part of your system of defense. Its purpose is to allow you to be able to focus on a threat with increased visual acuity, thereby increasing your chances for overcoming the attack. And it can do this very well. But the disadvantages that tunnel vision can create, by leaving you more vulnerable to attacks from other angles, and less critically, by affecting your later recollection of events, must be considered.

So how can you control tunnel vision? You may not be able to stop tunnel vision from occurring under high stress, but you can "break" tunnel vision. When faced with a high stress situation resulting in tunnel vision, if you look from side to side, moving your head instead of just your eyes, you can stop the effects of tunnel vision. You must remember not to try this until you can do it safely. In other words, tunnel vision is the result of a very real threat, and it may be better to neutralize the initial threat that brought on the tunnel vision before looking in other directions.

Tunnel vision is just one form of visual distortion that you may experience. Another one is a distortion of time and events usually referred to as the slow motion effect. If you experience this, everything will appear to be moving at an abnormally slow speed. This is really the result of your brain increasing the speed at which it processes the information received from your eyes, causing things to appear to slow down. So it is not truly a visual distortion, but that is how you will perceive it.

Officers who have experienced this type of distortion of time and events often describe things in great detail that would normally be indescribable because they happen much too fast to be seen by human eyes. A semiautomatic handgun, for example, when fired, goes through a cycle of ejecting a spent casing and seating a fresh round into the chamber as the slide moves backward and then forward in the blink of an eye. It happens much too quickly to be seen, yet under the effects of extreme stress, officers have not only seen it, they have described it after the fact in great detail.

Often times, officers who have experienced this will describe a higher level of confidence in their ability to control the situation than they would have expected. The seemingly slow speed that seems to prevail makes the officer feel as if he has plenty of time to take whatever action is necessary to neutralize the threat. Of course, you should remember that it is only a change in your perception that will occur, and that time does not actually slow down.

The main disadvantage, of course, is that if you experience distortion of time and events, you probably won't give a very accurate account of your experience after the fact. Your estimations of time relating to the incident will most likely be somewhat inaccurate. A well trained investigator will understand this, so the effects on your perception of events shouldn't be cause for alarm. You need only to be aware of the potential problems before you are faced with them.

Another effect you may experience is called auditory exclusion, sometimes referred to, somewhat inaccurately, as "tunnel hearing." Auditory exclusion will limit your ability to hear any or all sounds that occur during a traumatic event. Officers sometimes report that gunshots sound muffled during a gunfight, and sometimes they don't hear the shots at all. Other times they hear the gunshots, but voices or other sounds are muffled, or completely tuned out. Some officers hear nothing at all for the duration of the event.

Not hearing all, or part of, the sounds that occur during a critical situation can have the same disadvantages as tunnel vision. If you experience auditory exclusion, to any degree, you could miss important danger clues, such as an assailant approaching from behind. Or you might not hear another officer on the scene attempting to alert you to danger, or coordinate a tactical plan. And again, your recollection of the incident for reporting purposes will not be entirely accurate if you don't hear everything that was said, or all of the gunshots that were fired, during a gunfight.

Your vision and hearing are not the only things that can be affected by sudden fear or high stress. Your manual dexterity is also susceptible. Remember that when the body prepares for fight or flight the blood is redistributed from the skin and viscera to the muscles and brain. This redistribution of blood away from the skin can lead to a loss of fine motor movement. Fine motor movements such as operating the magazine release on a semiautomatic handgun, or inserting a key into a shotgun lock, can become more difficult under stress.

There are two ways to combat this. The first is to minimize the use of fine motor skills involved in training. Gross motor movements should be substituted for fine motor skills whenever possible. This is why many firearms instructors avoid the use of the slide release when teaching reloading skills. If a semiautomatic handgun is emptied while shooting, and the slide locks to the rear, the empty magazine must be removed and a full magazine inserted. Once the fresh magazine is inserted, the slide must be allowed to move forward in order to chamber a round. If you do this by using your thumb to operate the slide release, you are using a fine motor skill that may not be as efficient under stress. But if you grasp the rear portion of the slide, using your whole hand, and pull it back slightly to release the slide lock, you can then release the slide and allow it to move forward and chamber a round. And in doing so, you will be using gross motor movements, which are much more reliable under stress.

The second option is simply to be mentally prepared for the effects of sudden fear or high stress so that you can avoid as much inefficiency as possible. First, if you are know ahead of time that your fine motor skills can be affected under stress, you can prepare yourself by practicing those fine motor movements that cannot be substituted with gross movements in training. Second, you can use stress relieving techniques, such as deep breathing, to calm yourself down in a high stress situation if you are having difficulty with a task that requires fine motor skills.

Remember that in a life or death situation, you will want all of your skills to be as practiced, and efficient, as possible. And there are certain skills that you will be able to adapt to gross motor movements, and some that you will not. But by simply being aware of the potential for a loss of dexterity, you can prepare for it in case it happens to you, so you will not be surprised by it.

Additionally, you should practice your physical skills, such as reloading, under the most realistic of conditions. For example, you should not wait for a nice warm summer day to go to the shooting range. You should practice in the rain and in the snow. You should practice in the daytime and in the dark of night. If you wear gloves during the winter months, you should practice your firearms skills while wearing them. You won't be allowed the privilege of choosing the weather and lighting conditions when you are involved in a shooting, so why would you practice only under ideal conditions? You shouldn't. You should practice under all conditions, so that you will not have to try to adjust to adverse conditions for the first time when you are under stress.

There are many things that you can experience under extreme stress. If you become involved in a critical incident, you may experience some, all, or none, of the effects that I've just discussed. Not everyone experiences the same effects of stress, and not everyone experiences the effects equally. You may experience any number of the different effects, and to any degree. The important thing to remember about them is that they *can* happen. If you experience any of them, it won't mean that you "freaked out", or lost control, or anything of the sort. It's simply the normal reaction of your body and your mind to high stress.

Do not dwell too much on whether or not it will happen to you, or how it will affect your performance, if you are faced with a life threatening encounter. Just be aware of the fact that it can happen, and what the effects might be, so that you can be prepared. Just as in other areas of survival that I've discussed, you don't want to be taken by surprise by the effects of sudden and extreme stress. The better prepared you are for a critical incident, the better you will be able to handle the situation, both during and after.

There is one effect of sudden stress that can be very beneficial to you. In fact, it has no disadvantages whatsoever. In most cases, under stress you will instinctively revert to the way that you have been trained. Of course, in order for this to be beneficial to you, you must train properly and you must train often. This is what has often been described by those who have experienced it as "auto-pilot."

When faced with sudden stress, you will instinctively react in the way that you have been trained. And even though you will go through an entire thought process and make conscious decisions as to how you will respond to a threat, it will probably happen so fast that it will seem automatic. This is because you have practiced and mentally rehearsed so much that you do not have to think about your training. You know what action is necessary, and you take it without hesitation. This is yet another reason to take training seriously, and to practice often.

Because of the fact that under stress you will instinctively revert to the way you have been trained, there is something else you need to consider when training. That something is known as "muscle memory." Muscle memory is your body's natural tendency to learn movements that are repeated often, and to perform these same movements in an identical fashion time after time. For example, suppose you carry a wallet in your right hip pocket everyday. When you need your wallet, you don't have to think about where it is. Your hand moves naturally to that pocket, sometimes before you are even aware of it. This is because you have carried your wallet in the same place for weeks, months, or even years, and your right hand naturally reaches to the same place every time you need it.

Now suppose that you start carrying your wallet in your left hip pocket. Try it. If you always carry your wallet, or a comb, or your keys, or some other object that you carry everyday, in the same pocket, try moving it to another location. Then notice what happens the first time you need it. You will find yourself reaching for it in its previous location, and you'll have to stop and remind yourself that it's now in a different place.

So how does this apply to training? Imagine that you decide after several years as a street officer, to try a plainclothes position. And to go along with your new position, you buy a new holster - a shoulder holster. You have been training your body, through countless repetitions during your time in a uniformed position, to reach for your weapon at the location on your duty belt where it is normally carried. Now, your sidearm is off of your duty belt, and hanging from your shoulder. If you become involved in a shooting, muscle memory will cause you to reach for your weapon in its old location, and you will have to take the time to remind yourself that you moved it. And as I've mentioned before, you don't have that kind of time in a gunfight.

You can, of course, retrain your muscle memory to adapt to the new location of your sidearm, but this takes time. It can take thousands of repetitions to train your muscle memory. And you could become involved in a shooting while you're still trying to adapt. Going for your weapon in the wrong location could cost precious seconds even if you correct your movements during the incident. It would be much simpler if your body did not have to make that kind of adjustment in the first place.

You should make every effort to stick to one practical location for each piece of equipment that you carry, not just your sidearm. Under stress, you don't need to be thinking about where your are carrying your weapon, or your handcuffs, or anything else, for that matter. You may have much more important things to focus on, such as survival.

Under stress, you will revert to training.

*"Think of, and look at, your work as though it were done
by your enemy. If you look at it to admire it, you are lost."*
Samuel Butler (1835-1902), English author

8

Critique

Unfortunately, one of the main sources of education that we
must rely upon in law enforcement is our own troubled past.
Whenever a law enforcement officer is killed or injured in the
line of duty, the only real good that can come from such an
occurrence is for the rest of us to learn from any mistakes that
may have been made by the officer, so that, hopefully, we can
avoid making the same mistakes. It may seem morbid to study
the ways that officers die, but if we refuse to learn from their
mistakes, we will be doomed to repeat them.

Of course, we should study all critical incidents that officers
become involved in, without focusing solely on the incidents in
which officers are killed. We can learn just as much, if not
more, from those who have faced life and death situations and
survived. And perhaps even more valuable are the lessons to be
learned from those officers who survived despite being shot or
injured in some other way. Regardless of the outcome, there are
always lessons to be learned, based on both the proper survival
tactics that may have been used, and on the mistakes that may
have been made.

And officers do make mistakes. Sometimes the mistakes are
serious enough to get them injured or killed. In rare cases, law
enforcement officers are killed even when they do everything
tactically correct. Most officers that are killed, however, are
killed because they made a fatal error. Many times it is an error
that other officers have made before, but it did not prove fatal,

possibly due only to sheer luck. And because you are striving to become a tactical thinker, you will want to learn from these mistakes so that you do not depend on luck to survive.

When an officer is involved in a critical incident and lives to tell about it, many times he or she is more than willing to share the experience with the rest of us, mistakes and all, in the hope that we can all benefit. This is the ideal situation for turning a negative experience into a positive one. Anytime the person or persons who were actually involved in an incident are willing to discuss their experience for training purposes, the potential for learning is substantially increased. First, the details of the incident will be recounted with greater accuracy by someone who was actually involved, rather than facts routed through the convoluted system of the grapevine. Second, the person or persons involved will be able to relate more than what happened. They will be able to tell you why they made the decisions that they made, and whether they now consider those decisions right or wrong. They will also be able to tell you how they felt before, during, and after the incident.

Sadly enough, not all officers survive to tell about the critical incidents that they become involved in. In these cases, we stand to gain the most from turning the death of a fellow officer into a learning experience, as learning from his or her mistakes has the potential to keep us alive. But because the mistakes were fatal, we obviously cannot hear the details firsthand. Still, I prefer to believe that any officer who has been killed in the line of duty would want all of us to have the benefit of learning from his mistakes, just as if he had lived to tell about it himself.

It is very important that you understand there is a notable difference between the critique of an incident for the purposes of learning, and "Monday morning quarterbacking." "Monday morning quarterbacking" is nothing more than speculation or second guessing. It is usually based on a minimal amount of information, most of which is often times inaccurate. The source of the information is usually very unreliable, and the so-called facts are often relayed from person to person, becoming more and more distorted along the way.

When you hear about officers involved in a critical incident, whether or not the incident occurred in your jurisdiction, avoid the temptation to listen to, or become involved in, this type of speculation. It is unfair to the officers involved for you to evaluate their performance without the facts. In fact, even if you do have an accurate account of the details, it would still be unfair for you to pass judgment simply because you were not there.

So how can you learn from the mistakes of officers killed in the line of duty, and still pay them the respect they are due? The first thing to do is be sure you have **all** of the facts. Never try to evaluate an incident without all the pertinent information. Then, be sure to evaluate the incident only under the direction of a qualified instructor. This will help to insure that the session is a productive discussion of tactics and procedures. When conducted in a training environment, under the guidance of qualified instructors, and with all the pertinent facts, there is no reason why you should not be able to learn from the experiences of other officers. Just remember that you were not there, and unless you yourself have been involved in a life and death situation, you do not know for sure how you will react. (This is yet another good reason to practice your survival skills and mental rehearsal.)

Learning from the experiences of other officers is not the only way to use critique and evaluation to your advantage. As someone new to the job, you will make mistakes. In fact, you will make mistakes long after you graduate from rookie status. Hopefully, as you grow in your career, your mistakes will become fewer and less frequent. If they don't, it will be an indication that you are not learning from them. Of course the whole idea is to learn from your mistakes so that you don't repeat them.

When you are on patrol, you will be involved in a number of situations that you can learn from. In fact, any activity at all, from traffic stops to domestic disputes, can be used as an instructor, of sorts. All that is necessary is for you to take the time to evaluate your performance when the call is over. This should be done as soon as possible after the conclusion of the call, but you will not always have time to do it immediately. If you can't take the time to do some self critique after a call, you can always do it after your shift, while driving home or changing out of your uniform.

The important thing is to do it. Spend just a few minutes replaying the call in your mind, keeping in mind all of the tactical skills that you have been taught. Think about your approach to the call, both in your vehicle and on foot. Think about what you were thinking while you were making your approach. Were you alert to any danger clues that were present? Were you aware of the advantages or disadvantages of your position, such as cover or concealment? In dealing with subjects, did you take a position of advantage? How effective were your verbal skills? Were you able to have a calming effect, or were you antagonizing? Were you in control of the situation, or did you allow the people that you were dealing with to control the outcome? And so on, and so forth. There are endless questions that you can ask yourself to evaluate your performance.

When using self critique, be honest with yourself. If you think you made a mistake, own up to it. Don't subscribe to the theory that if you survived the call, you must have done everything right. If the call was violent, or potentially violent, and you survived, you probably did some things right, but you cannot automatically assume that you did *everything* right. You may have made some mistakes that for some reason had no negative impact on the outcome of the situation. It's important to recognize these mistakes and to be honest about what **could** have happened as a result. Then learn from your mistakes. Tell yourself that you will not let the same thing happen next time. And mean it.

Again, the most important thing is that you do some type of self critique, and if you feel there was anything at all you could have done differently, that may have produced a better result or reduced your chances for injury if the situation had gone bad, that you learn from it and apply it to your next experience. And you don't have to wait until after a particularly dangerous call to evaluate your own performance. You can critique yourself after any call that requires tactical thinking and the use of tactics. Traffic stops, building searches, domestic disputes; all can provide an excellent opportunity for self critique.

If you do have the opportunity to do self critique immediately following a call, this would be the most ideal time to do it. This is especially true if your are evaluating your performance at a call that was handled by more than one officer. In this case, it is always a good idea to spend a few minutes with whoever worked with you on the call, evaluating your performance both individually and as a team. This works well when you work with the same people on a regular basis, especially if you are comfortable with them. Of course, everyone taking part must be open to criticism. Spend just a few minutes talking about how the call was handled, and what you observed about your own performance and your partner's performance as well. You may observe something that your partner did or didn't do, that he did not notice, and vice versa.

When evaluating performance during a call it is very important to be sure that your focus is not solely on the mistakes that may have been made. You should make a concerted effort to take note of those things you did well on the call. This helps to reinforce your confidence in your abilities. This type of positive reinforcement should be remembered when you are doing critique with partners, also. Point out something to your partner that he did well. If you feel he did everything well, tell him.

By using self critique, and critique with your coworkers, you will be able to turn each day on the job into a learning experience. And even if you don't learn anything new from a day's work, you will be taking active measures to keep your survival attitude and tactics fresh in your mind. It will take longer to forget things that you learned in the academy; and if you do not have the opportunity to receive refresher training for a length of time, you can use your self evaluation as your own training sessions. Of course, if you are doing self critique and you feel there is something you could have done better, but you aren't sure exactly how to improve your performance for next time, you may have to refer to an officer survival textbook; or better yet, consult a qualified officer survival instructor.

Remember too, that when you do realize that you have made a mistake on a call, you should not dwell on it or beat yourself up over it. Everyone makes mistakes and you will be no exception. Learn from your mistakes; be proud of yourself when you do things right, and move on.

"To withdraw is not to run away; and to stay is no wise action, when there's more reason to fear than to hope."
Miguel de Cervantes (1547-1616), Spanish writer

9

Off Duty Survival

Should your survival attitude be any different when you are off duty? Well, for one thing, you may need to be even more alert. When off duty you will be interacting in the same environment that you are used to working in. The same crimes occur in the world whether you are in or out of uniform. Because of this, you need to be on your toes even when you aren't working. You never know when you'll find yourself unexpectedly forced to take action when you thought you had the day off.

The level of action that you take in an off duty encounter will depend on a number of things. One thing to consider is that when off duty you do not have the same resources available to you that you have when you are on duty. Back up will probably not be readily available; and even if it is close by, you won't have a portable radio handy to call for assistance. So you'll have to rely on the phone, or on someone else to summon help if necessary. Additionally, when off duty, you probably won't be carrying your usual assortment of equipment. You probably won't have a chemical agent or a baton, and you may or may not have handcuffs. You probably won't be wearing your body armor when you are off duty. As for your sidearm, whether or not you are carrying it will most likely depend, at least partially, on the policy of your agency.

So should you consider carrying all of your duty equipment when you're not working? You'll have a difficult time looking inconspicuous walking through your local shopping center wearing a duty belt with full gear, especially in the summertime when you may be wearing shorts or some other summer attire. But what about the individual pieces of equipment? Any baton other than an expandable baton is probably out of the question for off duty use. Full size batons, straight or side handle, are just too big to be concealed. Even expandable batons may pose difficulties in carrying and concealment.

Handcuffs can be heavy and bulky to carry out of uniform, but there are options. Handcuff manufacturers are making quality handcuffs from lighter materials, although not much can be done about the size of a good pair of cuffs. Several manufacturers offer thumb cuffs which can be used as a *temporary* solution when standard cuffs are not available, and they are small enough to slip easily into a pocket. Naturally, you should not use thumb cuffs until you have received the proper training. Flexible cuffs, or wire tie type cuffs may be a better solution for the off duty dilemma. They are lightweight and strong, and can be carried with relative ease. Again, be sure you have been properly trained in their use prior to carrying them.

Chemical agents are available in smaller containers than the standard duty size. They can easily be carried on a key ring, and they contain the same active ingredients as the larger canisters.

Your body armor is no more difficult to wear off duty than it is on duty. It may, however, be more difficult to conceal, depending on your attire. Whether or not you wear your body armor off duty is certainly your decision, but it is worth considering the fact that if you are carrying a firearm, you are carrying it to be prepared for a gunfight, and you can't be fully prepared for a gunfight without body armor.

As for your duty weapon, your agency will most likely have a policy that specifically governs off duty carrying. Some agencies prohibit it altogether, while others may mandate that you are armed at all times. Others may only *recommend* off duty carrying of a firearm. Still others may state in policy that carrying a firearm off duty is permitted, but they make no recommendation about it one way or the other. Of course, if you are carrying a firearm off duty, it should be concealed. This too, may depend on your agency's policy regarding off duty carrying of a sidearm. Still, concealed carry would be the most prudent choice if possible.

It can sometimes be difficult to conceal a handgun, but every effort should be made to conceal it effectively. Carrying it concealed offers you the advantage of being able to keep your identity as a law enforcement officer hidden until you choose to make it known. If you carry your firearm in the open for all to see, you will lose the element of surprise, which can be very valuable in an off duty situation.

Another option available to you when it comes to carrying equipment off duty is to carry minimal equipment on your person and keep the rest in your vehicle. Of course, you must remember that even in your vehicle, equipment will not always be readily accessible, as you will not always be in or near your vehicle when off duty. But if the choice is to carry equipment in your vehicle, where it may be available to you, or to not carry it at all, the decision is obvious.

Another consideration in determining what action to take if faced with an off duty crime is the overall situation. You must consider all of the circumstances before you decide to act. What type of crime is being committed? Is it a violent crime, such as a robbery? Or is it a property crime, such as a burglary? The difference is that if you are witnessing a violent crime in progress, the safety of innocent citizens is most likely in danger. On the other hand, if you are witnessing a suspect breaking into an unoccupied vehicle, there is probably no immediate danger to civilians. But there may be a significant amount of danger to you if you decide to intervene. In this case, the best thing for you to do may be to simply call for assistance and then observe the criminal activity until sufficient help arrives to handle the situation safely. In other words, be a good witness.

You also need to consider the safety of other people in the area, who may not be involved, but might be placed in harm's way should the situation deteriorate to the point of violence, such as gunfire. Take bank robberies for example. If you are in a bank during your off hours, and someone decides to hold up the place, you will have to decide if you should try to stop the robbery from occurring; or if you should let the robber do his thing and then take action after he has left the building. I can't tell you which is the correct decision because each situation is unique. You will have to decide, based on whether or not you feel that the customers in the bank will be safer if you let the robbery occur; or if you try to stop it. If you intervene, you may be the catalyst for a gunfight; and there are not many places that would be worse for a gunfight than the crowded lobby of a bank. If you don't take action, the bank robbers may hurt someone in the bank, and you may have been able to stop it. Perhaps your best option would be to allow the robbery to continue until you believe that intervention is necessary to protect yourself or someone else from imminent danger. The decision is yours, but you will have to decide quickly, taking into account the totality of the circumstances.

Additionally, you must remember that the way you are dressed off duty can work against you. I'm talking about those things that will let everyone know at first glance that you're a law enforcement officer. You will no doubt be proud of the fact that you have joined the force, as well you should be. Law enforcement is an honorable profession. But you should resist wearing t-shirts, or ball caps, with law enforcement slogans, or department insignia. Your ability to maintain the element of surprise will be lost if you're wearing these things. You may as well be in uniform. Anything that easily identifies you as an officer should be avoided.

Not only does this type of attire let everyone who sees you know that you're an officer, you may forget that you are wearing your favorite department t-shirt. Therefore, you may think you have the element of surprise on your side, when in fact the suspects in the crime have already picked you out of the crowd and recognized you as a potential threat to the completion of their task. Never assume that just because you are off duty, no one can recognize you as an officer.

The other side of the coin is that if you become involved in an off duty encounter, the responding officers may have no way of telling you apart from the suspect, or suspects. And mistaken identity can prove fatal, especially if you have a gun in your hand. Those department t-shirts and caps still won't work in your favor, however, because a good street officer will require more tangible proof that you are who you say you are when you're wearing civilian clothes, and you're carrying a handgun. Be prepared to identify yourself to the on duty officers who are dispatched to assist you. Don't expect them to know who you are. You will probably have to show them your badge or department I.D. when they arrive.

There's also the possibility of being confronted off duty by someone that you have arrested in the past. You will arrest many people during the course of your career, and you most likely won't remember them all. But they will remember you. So you have to be alert to people looking at you as if they recognize you from somewhere but they're not quite sure from where. Of course, you should not assume that everyone you arrest will immediately want to start trouble the first time they see you. Most will probably not even approach you. And how they think of you will depend partly on how they were treated by you when you arrested them. If you treat people with respect, they will most likely remember that. And they won't have a reason to want to get even with you.

Naturally, there will always be those people who will despise you because you are an officer, an authority figure, regardless of how well you have treated them. But if you treat all people with respect, you will decrease your chances of being confronted with a dissatisfied customer during your off hours.

Overall, you're going to have to think of yourself as being on duty all the time. But, as I mentioned earlier, you have to be careful not to let the job take over your life. It can be a difficult balance sometimes. You have to be able to relax enough to enjoy your time off. At the same time you have to stay alert to the dangers of the street, so that you can do your job if you find yourself unexpectedly pressed into service.

One way to prepare yourself for the possibility of an off duty confrontation is to use mental rehearsal. Just as mental rehearsal can prepare you for violent situations on duty, it can be helpful in preparing for off duty conflicts as well. Ask yourself as you are walking into that bank to cash your paycheck, on your day off; "What if....?" Then go over different scenarios in your mind. Then change them around and go over them again. If nothing else, it may keep you from being bored as you wait in line. But don't get lost in your daydreams, or you may not be alert to danger if it does make an appearance. And again, don't become so overly concerned about being confronted off duty that you can't relax and enjoy your time off.

Remember, on duty or off duty, the rule is: Awareness, not paranoia.

"We are not interested in the possibilities
of defeat; they do not exist."
Victoria (1819-1901), Queen of Great Britain and Ireland

10

Never Say Die

A major component in your survival attitude is your determination to win, regardless of the odds. You must make the commitment to survive. You have to make the decision that if violently attacked, you will survive; no matter what it takes. You may be outnumbered, or out-gunned. You may be up against an assailant that is much larger than you, or highly trained in hand-to-hand or weapon skills. You may even be shot, or injured in some other way. None of these things matter. You can survive a gunfight, a violent attack, and even being shot if you are determined enough.

Don't misunderstand me. You are not superhuman. Your badge, sidearm, and body armor do not make you invincible. However, you are probably quite a bit tougher than you think. And your body is much more resistant to injury than you might believe. If you are like many people new to law enforcement, your only experience in regard to the effects of gunshot wounds comes from the most unreliable source of all - television. On television, when someone is shot, the effectiveness of the weapon used against that person is usually directly related to the importance of the character who is being shot. In other words, the star of the show may be shot every week and never even require time off work to recuperate. The bad guys on the show, on the other hand, are usually sent flying backwards through the air from the impact of a single bullet, and die on the scene.

In reality, people do not fly through the air when shot, and the possibility of surviving a gunshot wound depends on several different factors, including how prepared, and determined you are to survive. You must understand that if you are shot, it doesn't mean that you will die. Many people, law enforcement officers included, have been shot and have lived to tell about it. Officers have survived even after having been shot in vital areas, such as the heart or the head. Some have even survived multiple gunshot wounds.

Remember the changes that your body goes through when faced with sudden fear or high stress. These physiological changes are designed to protect you from harm. If you are injured, your body has already made adjustments to help decrease the negative effects of the injury on your body. But if you are shot, and you believe that you are going to die, you may go into shock. And if you go into shock, your chances of survival can actually decrease, even if the injury is not all that serious.

Gunshot wounds are not the only type of injury you may have to deal with. You could be subjected to injuries from an edged weapon, such as a knife or a razor blade. Or you could be struck by an impact weapon such as a baseball bat, or a tire iron. The type of weapon that you are confronted with is irrelevant to your survival attitude. You can survive the attack.

To complicate matters, if you are injured in an attack, you not only have to be determined enough to survive despite your injuries, you must have the drive to continue the fight if you are still in danger. In some cases, when an officer is attacked, the assailant immediately stops the attack when the officer is down. His goal at that point becomes escape, and he leaves without doing any more harm to the officer. But not always. You may be faced with a situation in which you are injured, but that is not enough for your assailant. He may intend to fight to the death. His intent may be to kill you.

So despite your injuries, and despite the fact that you may be getting tired, you will have to continue the fight. And you will have to keep on fighting for as long as it takes to stop the attack. This brings up another good reason to practice your physical skills, such as your defensive tactics and firearms skills. The more practiced you are, the faster you will be able to stop a violent attack.

Using whatever means are reasonable and necessary, you must stop your assailant's actions. You will learn during your academy training, or basic training, what is reasonable and necessary force, based on the totality of the circumstances in a given situation. But remember that what we're talking about is a violent attack, and your life may be in danger. If you believe that your life is in imminent danger, you will have to do everything in your power to ensure that you survive.

As I mentioned earlier when discussing mental rehearsal, it is important to include the possibility that you may be injured in an attack, when practicing mental rehearsal. This will prove to be critical in your ability to develop a strong survival instinct. If you never prepare for the chance that you may have to fight for your life after being injured, you may have a more difficult time continuing the fight. You may be tempted to give up. But if you prepare for the possibility, you will be more prepared for it if it happens. You will be more likely to continue to fight because you have already made up your mind that you're going to survive, whether you are injured or not.

Here again, you are better off simply because you are mentally prepared. This is another example of how allowing yourself to be surprised by an attack can be detrimental to the outcome. Your attacker will not be negatively affected as a result of being surprised by the attack. He will most likely be the one to initiate the attack. In other words, he will have a plan. So there's no reason for him to be surprised if the situation turns violent. As for you, if you are on your toes, prepared for an attack, you may be able to take control of the situation before your assailant even has the opportunity to put his plan into action. At the very least, you will be ready, and not taken by surprise if an attack does occur. Now you have improved your chances of surviving the attack, because your focus is on your goal of stopping your assailant's actions, rather than on dealing with the surprise of being attacked. Because even if you are only *momentarily* distracted by the surprise of a sudden, violent attack, an awful lot can happen in those few moments.

When you are violently attacked, you may even have to take actions that go against your natural instincts, in order to increase your chances of survival. For example, suppose you are assaulted with a firearm while conducting a traffic stop. As you exit your vehicle, the driver jumps from the car and points a handgun at you. Your natural instincts may tell you to turn back to your vehicle and call for help on the radio. Or perhaps your instincts will tell you to run to cover and get out of the line of fire. These may not be the best options for survival.

Many officers have been shot while attempting to get out of the line of fire, or while attempting to call for help. Moving to cover, or trying to return to your vehicle for any reason should only be done when you can do it tactically, that is, when you can do it without leaving yourself vulnerable to the attack. Don't think of your vehicle as your safe haven, or your radio as your lifeline. If your retreat won't be tactical, don't retreat at all. Engage your attacker and stop the attack.

Your primary concern when faced with a violent confrontation such as this, should be to neutralize the attacker as quickly as possible. Of course, cover and communications are as important as always, and I don't mean to discount that. But it's important to remember that there is a time to call for help, a time to move to cover, and there is a time to stop the attack.

Think about your assailant's intentions when he attacks. His focus will be on carrying out the attack. If you turn and try to get out of the line of fire, you will have done nothing to change his focus. On the other hand, if you take the offensive and launch a counterattack, you will force him to change his focus from an attack posture to a defensive one. This may be enough to either stop the attack, or put you in a position to end the attack. Ideally, you should take offensive and defensive actions simultaneously so that you are minimizing your chances of injury from your assailant's actions, and forcing your assailant to change his focus, and thus his plan, at the same time. An example of this would be returning fire at your assailant while moving to cover. In order to be able to do this effectively however, you will have to acquire training specifically designed to teach you how to shoot on the move. And then of course, practice, practice, practice. Naturally, the decision to move, shoot, or shoot on the move will be yours, and you won't have all day to think about it.

No matter what happens, the will, and determination, to survive are the very essence of the survival attitude. Without the genuine determination to survive, all the other elements of the survival attitude are meaningless. In fact, all the other components of your survival attitude will be based on your determination to survive. If you do not have a real will to survive, you will not take the development of your survival attitude seriously. You will not practice the fundamentals of each aspect of the survival attitude often enough for them to be beneficial to you. And a good survival attitude *must* be maintained. It must be practiced continuously in order for it to be maintained and so it may continue to develop.

I use the words "real" and "genuine" in describing the survival attitude because it is not enough to simply *say* that you will survive. You have to mean it. You have to believe it. And you have to live it. The way that you approach your job, whether you're on the street, in the office, or in the classroom, should reflect your survival attitude.

If you have a genuine will to survive, you will take every aspect of the job seriously. You will take all training seriously because you know there is a chance that what you learn in training may one day save your life. And you won't forget that. You will constantly and consistently evaluate the risks involved in your daily activities and recognize the level of danger that is, or may be, present. You will never underestimate your potential adversaries.

And so, when faced with sudden and extreme violence, you will be ready. You will not be surprised. You will be mentally and physically prepared to do whatever is necessary for survival. You won't hesitate, and if you are afraid, you won't be controlled by your fear. You will be proficient in your tactical and physical skills. You will revert to your training, and do exactly as you have been trained to do. You will use proper tactics and techniques, because you have practiced and mentally rehearsed them. And above all, you will refuse to give up, no matter what. You will continue to fight until you have taken control of the situation and stopped the attack, even if you are injured. And you will continue to survive even after the fight is over. You will not succumb to your injuries. You will not allow yourself to give in to your wounds after having fought so hard to survive. That would simply be another form of defeat. And you cannot allow yourself to be defeated. You have too much to live for, and there are too many people counting on you.

So regardless of the type of weapons being used, if any, or the number of attackers you are confronted with, if you are violently attacked, you must maintain a fierce determination to survive. **No matter what happens, you will not give up.** You cannot afford to. If you give up, you are dead. But if you refuse to give up, you will survive. You will live to go home and see your family. You will live to see another day on the job. And you will live to see your attacker brought to justice (if he survived).

"The problems of victory are more agreeable than the problems of defeat, but they are no less difficult."
Sir Winston Churchill (1874-1965), British statesman, writer

11

When It's Over

You will train and practice and prepare for the day when you may be forced to shoot someone in defense of your life or someone else's life. And then it happens. If you are properly prepared for the incident, you will survive. But then, what next?

Next to your physical survival, your emotional survival is the most important reason to develop your survival attitude. Because following involvement in a critical incident, such as a shooting, will be many factors directly related to your level of preparation. Let's examine some of the things related to your survival attitude that you may experience after a shooting.

First of all, if you have properly prepared yourself for involvement in a shooting, you will feel less shock when it actually happens. Shock is not necessarily a bad thing. It's your body's way of absorbing the impact of a traumatic event a little bit at a time, in order to keep you from being overwhelmed by the reality of what you have been through. Even so, if you are properly prepared for a critical incident you may feel less initial shock; and therefore, you may be better able to continue to do your job well, after the fact. This can be beneficial in the moments immediately following the shooting when you are tasked with the responsibility of securing the scene, rendering aid, and all of the other things that you will have to take care of until someone else arrives and takes over for you. It can also help during the investigation that will follow. And it can help you deal with any other stress you may feel, as you will feel more like yourself if you are not in shock.

Something else worth considering is self-critique. Whether or not you practice self-critiquing on a regular basis will probably be irrelevant to whether or not you practice it after a critical incident. When you become involved in a shooting you may spend quite a bit of time going over the incident in your mind, asking yourself if you did everything right, or if there is anything that you could have done better, or differently, that would have produced a better outcome. There is nothing wrong with this, as you can learn just as much from critiquing your performance during a violent encounter as you can from any other incident, and perhaps even more.

The important thing is not to let yourself become obsessed or preoccupied with the incident. But initial evaluation of your performance will probably be something you will most likely be compelled to do. This is another critical area in which the importance of your survival attitude will come into play. Because the better you have practiced and prepared for involvement in a shooting, the better your performance is likely to be. And the better your performance, the easier it may be for you to cope with any critical incident stress that you may experience as a result of the incident.

Yes, officers can experience stress related to shootings. And no, there's absolutely nothing wrong with that. Becoming involved in a shooting can be very stressful for anyone. Officers can experience any number of stress related symptoms such as sleeplessness, nightmares, changes in eating habits, changes in sex drive, and so on. It's perfectly normal to experience these symptoms in any combination, including experiencing none of them at all. Your body will be reacting in normal ways to abnormal circumstances. But this kind of stress reaction can't take you by surprise if you are expecting it. You should study critical incident stress, either through classes taught by qualified instructors, or by reading every text on the subject that you can find. Study it before you become involved in a shooting. And then ask your loved ones to study it as well. If they understand ahead of time what you may be going through after a critical incident, they can be prepared for it also.

But let's get back to the survival attitude. As you evaluate your performance under fire, you will be better able to cope with any resulting stress if you are satisfied with the way you handled the situation. Consider too, that the worse the outcome, the greater the stress may be. Not all shootings are as simple as a suspect pointing a weapon at, or shooting at, an officer and being killed as a result. There is always the possibility that you could be seriously injured in the course of the events. And even though you will survive, your injuries could drastically change your life. You could be injured seriously enough to be forced to retire from law enforcement. But if you did everything that you could have possibly done to prevent yourself from being injured, you may have one less stress-inducing factor to contend with. In other words, it will be much more difficult to blame yourself for your injuries if you could not have prevented them.

And what about the possibility that another officer on the scene could be seriously injured or killed? Or perhaps an innocent civilian is injured or killed during the gunfire, and you were unable to prevent it. These are the kinds of things that will cause you to take an even harder look at your performance. And if you can find no fault in your actions, you will probably find it easier to cope with the stress of the incident.

This is not to say that if the outcome of the incident is not flawless that you will be unable to cope with the resulting stress. You can most likely handle whatever stress you may experience relatively well considering what you have been through. It just might be easier if you don't have these extra factors to complicate the issue. Again, plan, practice, and be prepared for the worst; and you will be better able to deal with it when it happens.

One way to help to prepare yourself for a shooting is to include scenarios with less than desirable outcomes in your mental rehearsal. Include scenarios in which another officer is injured or killed. Or include scenarios in which an innocent civilian is injured or killed. Then ask yourself when you are through with your mental rehearsal how you would deal with that if it actually happened. By doing this you can keep yourself from being caught off guard if you are involved in a shooting and the outcome is not a happy one. And the chances of you being involved in such an incident are real. They are real because you do not have control over anyone's tactics, other than your own. And you may not be able to adequately control the actions of all civilians at the scene either, regardless of how hard you try. A civilian or another officer may take some action that places them in an unsafe position, and leads to serious consequences. It may be out of your control, but you will have to deal with it nonetheless.

Of course, some will say that there is no way to fully prepare for such an occurrence. It's true. You have no real idea what it is like to be involved in a critical incident until you have experienced it. But that doesn't mean that preparation is not helpful. You can still prepare yourself for the fact that it can happen to you. And you can prepare your family for the possibility.

Following a shooting you will, at some point, have to return to duty and face the possibility of becoming involved in another critical incident. You must understand that your chances of being involved in another shooting do not decrease after your being involved in one. In fact, just the opposite may be true. No good law enforcement officer wants to shoot anyone; and after you have experienced it, you will probably hope against hope that you never have to do it again. But if you want to stay in law enforcement, you must accept the fact that it can happen all over again.

When you are new to law enforcement, it is very important to ask yourself if you could take a life in the line of duty if you had to in order to defend your life, or the life of someone else. If you cannot honestly answer ''yes'' to this question, you have no business becoming a law enforcement officer. Because you may find yourself in a situation where human life is dependent on your ability to pull the trigger. If you hesitate, you could cost someone his life.

After becoming involved in a shooting, it is just as important to ask yourself this question all over again. Because your life and the lives of others may be placed in your hands. Other officers are depending on you. So before you return to duty, ask yourself if you can do it again if you have to. The answer will most likely be ''yes'' because you will most likely find that although being involved in a shooting can be stressful, and you hope that you don't have to do it again, you have worked hard to become a good officer, and there will be absolutely no reason to give all that up.

So once again, prepare yourself well for the day when you will be faced with a life and death situation. Do not allow yourself to fall into the trap of thinking that you will deal with it when it happens. If you don't prepare mentally for it, you will be much more vulnerable to the after effects of such a traumatic experience. And worse, if you don't prepare yourself physically and tactically, you may not even survive.

"My art and profession is to live."
Michel de Montaigne (1533-92), French essayist.

In conclusion

There you have it. You are well on your way to becoming a tactical thinker. The key now is to continue to develop your survival attitude. Read every officer survival related book and magazine article that you can get your hands on. And if you like what you read, use it. Do not fall into the trap of complacency that can be very tempting, especially after several years on the job. Remember that you are just as likely to be assaulted on your last day on the job as you are on your first day.

Whatever you do during your career, never stop developing your survival attitude. Make the commitment to never stop learning. Make the commitment to always think tactically, to use good tactics, and to be a survivor. Do it for yourself, and do it for those who depend on you to return home at the end of each shift. For no matter who you are or who you work for, there will always be someone who cares about you and worries about you when you are working. It may be your spouse, or significant other. It may be your children. It may be your mother and father, and your siblings. Whoever it is, think about how they would be affected by your death, and do it for them. Whatever your motivation for maintaining your survival attitude, you must make the commitment and stick to it.

Remember, your life is at stake.

Bibliography

1) *Street Survival: Tactics for Armed Encounters*
   Adams, McTernan, and Remsberg
   Calibre Press   copyright 1980

2) *Horror, Fright and Panic*
   Hyde & Forsyth
   Walker Publishing Co.   copyright 1977

3) *The Psychology of Fear and Stress*
   Jeffrey A. Gray
   McGraw-Hill Book Co.   copyright 1971

4) *Science and Sanity: An Introduction to Non-Aristotelian Systems and General Semantics*
   Alfred Korzybski
   International Non-Aristotelian Library
                                                            copyright 1933

5) *Language in Thought and Action: Symbol, Status, and Personality*
   Samuel Ichiye Hayakawa
   Harcourt Brace Jovanovich   copyright 1963

6) *Eye Witness Testimony: Civil and Criminal*
   Second edition, Loftus & Doyle
   The Michie Company   copyright 1992

7) *The Nature and Conditions of Learning*
   Howard L. Kingsley
   Prentice-Hall, Inc.   copyright 1957

8) *The Effect of Mental Rehearsal and Mental
    Preparation on Confidence and Performance in a
    Physical Task*
    Jean Whitehead
    Unpublished thesis   1970

9) *Mental Preparation Strategies and Peak Performance
    Among Intercollegiate Baseball Players: An
    Exploratory Study*
    Thomas R. George
    Unpublished thesis   1988

10) *A Comparison of Traditional Instruction, Mental
    Practice, and Combined Physical-Mental Practice
    Upon the Learning of Selected Motor Skills*
    Robert C. LaLance Jr.
    Unpublished thesis   1974

11) *The Columbia Dictionary of Quotations*
    Columbia University Press   copyright 1993

12) *Killed in the Line of Duty*
    U.S. Department of Justice
    Federal Bureau of Investigation   1992

13) *Law Enforcement Officers Killed and Assaulted*
    U.S. Department of Justice
    Federal Bureau of Investigation   1993

PROTECT YOURSELF
HELP THE ONES YOU LOVE!

Problems in a relationship?
Things getting out of control?

THE DOMESTIC VIOLENCE
SURVIVAL GUIDE

A thought-provoking, option-packed guide on how to
Recognize, Prevent, Terminate and Survive
an encounter with
Relationship Abuse and Domestic Violence

- Build Self-Confidence
- Demand Respect
- Feel Secure
- Take Control
- Gain Freedom

Contains a new and unique approach to an old and confounding problem and is packed with positive, time-tested tactics and new strategies for survival.

Written by Cliff Mariani, veteran New York City
police officer, prominent author of
police training/promotion publications.

Edited by Patricia A. Sokolich, Attorney at Law,
Co-President of the *Queens Women's Center*, Founder and
Director of the *QWC's Legal Clinic for Women in Crises*.

This Guide offers a crash course on self-preservation

A Must-Have for:
Victims of abuse and their loved ones,
criminal justice personnel, social service workers,
and all those who may be called upon to act as counsellors

GET A COPY FOR YOURSELF OR A FRIEND IN NEED

Remember: *No one deserves to be abused!!*

Part One: RELATIONSHIPS	Part Four: HELP ARRIVES
After an informative **Orientation**, you'll be given a helpful lesson on the **Recognition** of abusive tendencies in both new and established relationships, followed by a concise discourse on **Prevention** techniques.	In serious or persistent cases of abuse, a police investigation may result in the **Apprehension** of the abuser and **Prosecution** through the court. We'll guide you through the "system."
Part Two: ABUSE BEGINS	Part Five: TIME FOR CLOSURE
For those persons beyond the benefits of early recognition and prevention, we shall focus on **Victimization**, along with civil and criminal **Legislation** and the **Origination** of procedural issues relating to the court system.	Chapters on **Diversion**, **Incarceration** and **Rehabilitation** reveal how the "system" can benefit the abused and the abuser by ending the violence.
Part Three: HELP AVAILABLE	Part Six: TURNING POINT
At a certain point in an abusive relationship, **Protection** is required, **Intervention** becomes necessary, and **Representation** is advisable. All three of these topics are covered.	**Conciliation** may be an option in limited cases. We'll explain. **Termination**, and its stay-go dilemma, is discussed in careful detail. **Recuperation**, our concluding chapter, can be your gateway to ultimate survival.

Please send _____ copy(ies) of **The Domestic Violence Survival Guide** (Softcover Edition - 5 1/2 x 8 1/2 - Over 200 pages), at a cost of **$19.95** per copy plus postage & handling and sales tax. This is a pre-publication notice, anticipated availability September 1996.

Quantity Discounts Available!

PLEASE PRINT CLEARLY

Name _____

Street Address _____ **Apt. No.** _____

Town & State _____ **Zip Code** _____

Daytime Phone Number (____) _____

	TOTAL COST OF ITEMS	$ _____
Postage & Handling (INSURED) ($4.00 for the first item, plus $3.00 for the second item and $2.00 for each item thereafter.		$ _____
Optional First Class ($3.00 extra per order)		$ _____
	Sales Tax ____ %	$ _____
	AMOUNT DUE:	$ _____

Credit Card #: _____
(M.C. / Visa / AMEX / Discover)   _____ (Expiration Date)

Telephone Orders by Credit Card or UPS-COD: (718) 359-5559

LOOSELEAF LAW PUBLICATIONS, INC. P.O. Box 650042, Fresh Meadows, N.Y. 11365-0042

Telephone: (718) 359-5559 *also* **24 Hour Fax No. (718) 539-0941**

The *Path* of the *Warrior*

AN ETHICAL GUIDE TO PERSONAL & PROFESSIONAL DEVELOPMENT IN THE FIELD OF CRIMINAL JUSTICE

By Larry F. Jetmore, Ph.D.,
Captain, Hartford PD, Ret.

Warriors are people who have chosen to walk a separate path, different from others. This book points the way to the path by sharing an ancient philosophy and code of honor used by *King Arthur's Knights of the Round Table, The French Foreign Legion, Navy Seals* and *Green Berets.* This book is written for and about those who have embraced the field of criminal justice as a way of life. It provides an ethical framework leading to personal development, growth, and professional success.

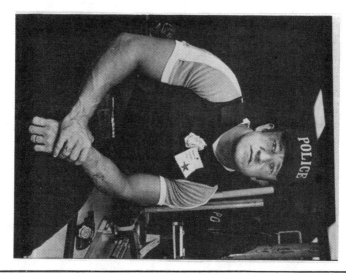

This book is written for police officers and students of law enforcement who are searching for practical ways to resolve the complicated ethical dilemmas faced by those who wear a badge and carry a gun.

People who have chosen policing as a way of life are especially vulnerable to a slow draining of enthusiasm and positive energy. In giving so much of themselves to others, over time it becomes increasingly difficult to rekindle the fire that first drew them to policing. This book offers a different way of thinking and living -- provides intervention techniques -- that many have found helpful in guarding their inner spirits while going where other fear to tread.

Answering the question, How does today's officer determine the 'right' thing to do? Is the primary focus of this work. We will explore different paths to taking positive control of our lives and stimulating personal and professional growth.

Please send _____ copy(ies) of *The Path of the Warrior* at a cost of **$19.95** per copy. I understand that if I am not totally satisfied I may return it (them) within 10 days for a full refund. I have enclosed payment as indicated below, including postage, tax and handling.

PLEASE PRINT CLEARLY

Quantity Discounts Available!

PLEASE PRINT CLEARLY

Name _____

Street Address _____ **Apt. No.** _____

Town & State _____ **Zip Code** _____

Daytime Phone Number

( ) _____

	TOTAL COST OF ITEMS	$ _____
Postage & Handling (INSURED) *($4.00 for the first item, plus $3.00 for the second item, and $2.00 for each additional item.)*		$ _____
Optional First Class *($3.00 extra per order)*		$ _____
Sales Tax _____ %		$ _____
AMOUNT DUE:		$ _____

Credit Card #: _____

_____
(Expiration Date)

RETURN THIS FORM WITH YOUR CHECK, PURCHASE ORDER OR VOUCHER TO:

LOOSELEAF LAW PUBLICATIONS, INC.

P.O. Box 650042, Fresh Meadows, N.Y. 11365-0042

Telephone Order by Credit Card (718) 359-5559 *also* **24 Hour Fax No. (718) 539-0941**

PROMOTION SERIES

(CIRCLE prices of items desired)

(CIRCLE prices of items desired)

Written Assessment Exercises For Police.	$21.95
Oral Assessment Exercises For Police.	$21.95
Management Quizzer.	$5.95
Pistol Instruction Handbook.	$6.95
Police Officer's Response Guide.	$29.95
Police Promotion Manual.	$15.95
Police Supervisor's Test Manual.	$21.95
Supervision Card Course.	$12.95
Supervisor's Interactive Computer Course (IBM Comp. Windows).	$19.95
The "HOW" of Criminal Law.	$6.95
The Domestic Violence Survival Guide.	$19.95

Civil Service Question Set (6 Books, postage = $5.00).	$24.95
1. Supervision.	$4.95
2. Administration.	$4.95
3. Personnel Management.	$4.95
4. Police Operations.	$4.95
5. Reading Comprehension.	$4.95
6. Communications.	$4.95
Emergency Responder's Pocket Field Guide.	$5.95
Speedy Spanish For Law Enforcement Personnel.	$4.95
Speedy Spanish For Medical Personnel.	$4.95
The New Dictionary of Legal Terms.	$10.95

TOTAL COST OF ITEM(s) $ _____

PLEASE PRINT CLEARLY

Name _____ **Daytime Phone #** _____

Postage & Handling (INSURED)
($4.00 for the first item plus
$3.00 for the second item
$2.00 for each item thereafter.
Publications costing $6.00 or less
add $2.50 per item.)

Street Address _____ **Apt.No.** _____

Optional First Class *($2.00 extra per order)* $ _____

Sales Tax _____% $ _____

City & State _____ **Zip Code** _____

AMOUNT DUE: $ _____

Telephone Orders by Credit Card or UPS - COD

Credit Card Number: *(M.C.- Visa - Discover - AMEX)* *(Exp. Date)*
_____

RETURN THIS FORM WITH YOUR CHECK, PURCHASE ORDER OR VOUCHER TO:

LOOSELEAF LAW PUBLICATIONS, INC.

P.O. BOX 650042, FRESH MEADOWS, N.Y. 11365-0042

or **41-23 150th Street, Flushing, N.Y. 11355**

Telephone: (718) 359-5559 *also* **24 Hour Fax No. (718) 539-0941**

A Summary of
U.S. Supreme Court
Decisions for the
Criminal Justice Community

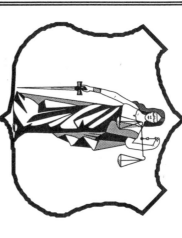

Over 125 United States Supreme Court Cases
of critical importance to law enforcement officers.

This book contains the summary of the opinion actually written by the Court's Reporter of Decisions. The accompanying *Windows* software contains the full report with dissenting and concurring opinions.

Searches	DWI	Entrapment	Use of Force
Civil Liability	Employment Rights	Exclusionary Rule	Warrantless Arrests
Confessions	Abandoned Property	Identification	Entry to Arrest
Probable Cause	Stop and Frisk	Sobriety Checkpoints	Search Warrants

and much, much more!

The book and software are subdivided according to topic and party name.

Easy-to-use software...look up decisions by party name, topic or conduct single or multiple word searches.

Use the copy and paste feature for report writing.

"A Summary of U.S. Supreme Court Decisions for the Criminal Justice Community"

Avoid costly liability actions...familiarize yourself with
the decisions that have the greatest impact on law enforcement.
Faced with today's legal issues...this book is a *MUST!*

Please send _____ copy(ies) of *A Summary of U.S. Supreme Court Decisions for the Criminal Justice Community* at a cost
of **$29.95** per copy. I understand that if I am not totally satisfied I may return it (them) within 10 days for a full refund. I have
enclosed payment as indicated below, including postage, tax and handling.

PLEASE PRINT CLEARLY

Quantity Discounts Available!

PLEASE PRINT CLEARLY

Name _____

Street Address _____ Apt. No. _____

Town & State _____ Zip Code _____

Daytime Phone Number
( ) _____

TOTAL COST OF ITEMS	$ _____
Postage & Handling (*INSURED*) (*$4.00 for the first item, plus $3.00 for the second item, and $2.00 for each additional item.*)	$ _____
Optional First Class (*$2.00 extra per order*)	$ _____
Sales Tax _____ %	$ _____
AMOUNT DUE:	$ _____

Credit Card #: _____

(M.C./Visa/AMEX/Discover)

_____
(Expiration Date)

RETURN THIS FORM WITH YOUR CHECK, PURCHASE ORDER OR VOUCHER TO:

LOOSELEAF LAW PUBLICATIONS, INC.

P.O. Box 650042, Fresh Meadows, N.Y. 11365-0042

Telephone Order by Credit Card (718) 359-5559 *also* **24 Hour Fax No. (718) 539-0941**

http://www.LooseleafLaw.com

Anyone with reason to read, write or interpret legal documents needs this handy dictionary!

THE NEW
DICTIONARY
OF
LEGAL TERMS
INCLUDES
CRIMINAL JUSTICE DATA TERMINOLOGY

By
IRVING SHAPIRO

Busy practitioners, paralegals, legal secretaries, court reporters and other court officials, law enforcement agents and law students need a quick and direct answer when they seek the meaning of a word. This dictionary is designed to fill that need.

Obsolete material has been screened out both to reflect the fluid quality of legal language and to emphasize terms and definitions in current use. The definitions employ simple words, requiring no further search for meaning.

Terms and definitions are included from the U.S. Bureau of Justice Statistics, ***Dictionary of Criminal Justice Data Terminology:*** Terms and definitions proposed for interstate and national data collection and exchange.

THE NEW DICTIONARY OF LEGAL TERMS

Only - $10.95

ABOUT THE AUTHOR: The dictionary is the work of Irving Shapiro, Professor of Criminal Justice and Court Management at St. John's University, New York. Professor Shapiro has been a member of the New York Bar for over 40 years. During part of this time he was a court official in New York courts during which time he lectured extensively and directed many training programs to prepare court personnel for competitive promotion examinations. His experience as a lawyer, court official, and teacher has given him a broad perspective for the design of a dictionary meeting the needs of the present day.

PLEASE PRINT CLEARLY

Name _____

Street Address _____ Apt.No. _____

Town & State _____ Zip Code _____

Telephone Orders by Credit Card or UPS - COD
(718) 359-5559

	TOTAL COST OF BOOKS	$ _____
Postage & Handling *(INSURED)*		
($4.00 for the first book plus		
$3.00 for the second book		
$2.00 for each book thereafter)		$ _____
Optional First Class *($2.00 extra per order)*		$ _____
Sales Tax _____ %		$ _____
AMOUNT DUE:		$ _____

Credit Card Number: _____ *(M.C./Visa/AMEX/Dis.)* _____ *(Expiration Date)*

RETURN THIS FORM WITH YOUR CHECK, PURCHASE ORDER OR VOUCHER TO:

LOOSELEAF LAW PUBLICATIONS, INC.

P.O. BOX 650042, FRESH MEADOWS, N.Y. 11365-0042

or **41-23 150th Street, Flushing, N.Y. 11355**

Telephone: (718) 359-5559 *also* **24 Hour Fax No. (718) 539-0941**